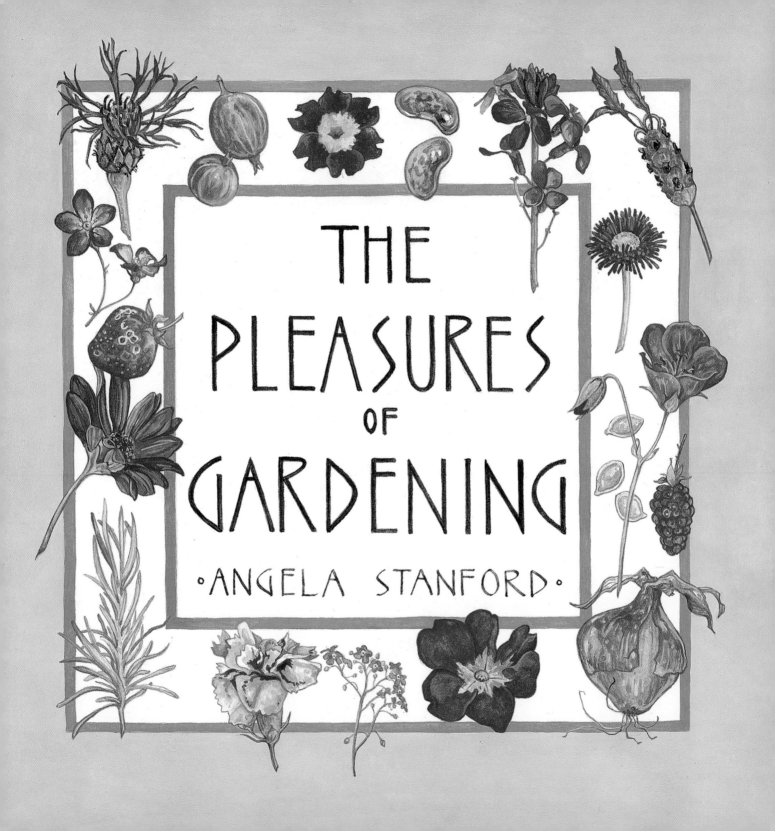

THE PLEASURES OF GARDENING

·ANGELA STANFORD·

THE PLEASURES
OF GARDENING

EBURY PRESS
LONDON

FIRST PUBLISHED IN GREAT BRITAIN IN 2001

1 3 5 7 9 10 8 6 4 2

EBURY PRESS
RANDOM HOUSE, 20 VAUXHALL BRIDGE ROAD, LONDON SW1V 2SA

RANDOM HOUSE AUSTRALIA PTY LIMITED
20 ALFRED STREET, MILSONS POINT, SYDNEY, NEW SOUTH WALES 2061, AUSTRALIA

RANDOM HOUSE NEW ZEALAND LIMITED
18 POLAND ROAD, GLENFIELD, AUCKLAND 10, NEW ZEALAND

RANDOM HOUSE (PTY) LIMITED
ENDULINI, 5A JUBILEE ROAD, PARKTOWN 2193, SOUTH AFRICA

THE RANDOM HOUSE GROUP LIMITED REG.NO. 954009

www.randomhouse.co.uk

PAPERS USED BY EBURY PRESS ARE NATURAL, RECYCLABLE PRODUCTS MADE FROM WOOD GROWN IN SUSTAINABLE
FORESTS

A CIP CATALOGUE RECORD FOR THIS BOOK IS AVAILABLE FROM THE BRITISH LIBRARY

ISBN 0 09 187863 2

PRINTED IN SINGAPORE

For my four wonderful
children,
Emmie, Liz, Henni & Tom
with love

I WOULD PARTICULARLY LIKE TO THANK
MARK LUCAS FOR THE IDEA,
JULIAN SHUCKBURGH FOR SAYING YES,
MY FRIENDS FOR HELPING WITH FLOWERS
AND BOOKS, AND MY FAMILY FOR THEIR
ENCOURAGEMENT.

·CONTENTS·

GOD ALMIGHTY FIRST
PLANTED A GARDEN;
AND, INDEED, IT IS THE
PUREST OF HUMAN
PLEASURE. IT IS THE
GREATEST REFRESH-
MENT TO THE SPIRITS
OF MAN.
FRANCIS BACON 1625

7

SPRING

BLOSSOM
BY BLOSSOM
THE
SPRING
BEGINS

SWINBURNE

SEASONAL TASKS

- STAKE TALL PERENNIALS AS GROWTH STARTS
- MULCH AND FEED EVERGREENS AND PERENNIALS
- SOW HERBS AND HALF HARDY ANNUALS IN GREENHOUSE
- PRUNE SPRING FLOWERING SHRUBS AFTER FLOWERING
- PRUNE LATE SUMMER FLOWERING SHRUBS LIKE BUDDLEIA
- DIVIDE PERENNIALS AS REQUIRED
- PRUNE ROSES
- FERTILIZE LAWN AND BEGIN MOWING REGULARLY
- WATCH OUT FOR SLUGS AND SNAILS
- PLANT SWEET PEAS IF NOT PLANTED IN THE AUTUMN
- PREPARE VEGETABLE BEDS AND START SOWING
- REMOVE WEEDS AS THEY APPEAR
- SOW GRASS SEEDS ONCE DAYS ARE WARMER

SPRING

Spring Bulbs

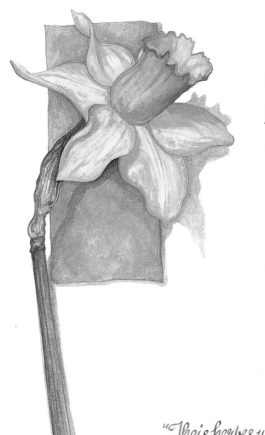

Choose plump firm bulbs and plant them during the autumn. Do not plant them in water-logged soil. Add grit as well if necessary under the bulbs so they do not rot. Most bulbs need to be covered with soil twice or three times their height and look at their best planted in irregular groups.

Daffodils, crocus, snowdrops & anemone blanda look good naturalized in grass. Throw the bulbs in the air and plant them where they fall. Forget about them until springtime! Most bulbs prefer a sunny spot, although bluebells, snowdrops and daffodils will happily flower in partial shade.

After flowering, dead head, feed and let the leaves die back. Do not tie the leaves in knots. After about 6 weeks when the leaves are yellow, cut back. Divide established groups of bulbs in early summer to improve flowering.

Daffodils should not be put with other cut flowers or they will poison them. Narcissus have been loved by man for many many centuries and were used in ancient Egyptian funeral wreaths. The juice of bluebells was used by the Elizabethans to stiffen muslin, paste books with and to attach feathers to arrows.

"Theis herbes which are set here under the name of Narcissus we calle Daffadowndylles. They be very common." W. Mount 1582

10

Muscari (GRAPE HYACINTH)

Eranthis (WINTER ACONITE)

Fritillaria (SNAKE'S HEAD FRITILLARY)

Scilla (SPRING SQUILL)

Erythronium (DOG'S TOOTH VIOLET)

Puschkinia (LEBANON SQUILL)

Anemone blanda (WINDFLOWER)

Chionodoxa (GLORY OF THE SNOW)

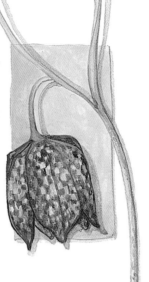

11

TULIPS WERE INTRODUCED TO EUROPE IN THE 16TH
CENTURY FROM TURKEY WHERE THEY GREW WILD. IN
1634-1637 HOLLAND WAS STRUCK BY TULIPOMANIA
WHEN BULBS OF STRIPED TULIPS WERE SOLD FOR
STARTLING AMOUNTS. ALTHOUGH IT TOOK YEARS BEFORE
THE COUNTRY RETURNED TO NORMALITY, THE DUTCH
STILL RETAIN THEIR LOVE FOR THIS STRIKING FLOWER.
NURSERY CATALOGUES IN ENGLAND PROUDLY LISTED
OVER 650 VARIETIES BY THE LATE 1700S. TODAY
THERE ARE OVER 5,000, OF MANY COLOURS & SHAPES,
~SINGLE, DOUBLE, PARROT, LILY, DARWIN AND SO ON.
DIFFERENT VARIETIES WILL EXTEND THE FLOWERING
SEASON TO SEVERAL MONTHS.

BULBS SHOULD BE FIRM AND PLUMP. PLANT BULBS
6" DEEP IN THE AUTUMN IN TUBS & BORDERS OR TO
NATURALIZE IN GRASS. TULIPS ENJOY A SUNNY PLACE
IN THE GARDEN. DEAD HEAD AFTER FLOWERING AND
LET THE LEAVES DIE DOWN BEFORE CUTTING BACK.

"THE TULIPE IS THE QUEENE OF BULBOUS PLANTS~
WHOSE FLOWER IS BEAUTIFUL IN ITS FIGURE, AND
MOST RICH AND ADMIRABLE IN COLOURS, AND
WONDERFUL IN VARIETY OF MARKINGS."
                        SIR THOMAS HANMER 1659
"WHEN THE PRINCIPAL OF THEM DISPLAY THEIR COLOURS
IN THE HEAT OF THE DAY THERE IS NOT A MORE GLORIOUS
SIGHT IN NATURE NOR IS IT TO BE IMITATED BY ART."
                        J. WORLIDGE 1677

13

PRIMULA AURICULA WAS ALSO CALLED 'BEAR'S EARES.' IN
REGENCY TIMES THEY WERE DISPLAYED IN AURICULA THEATRES,
ON SHELVING OFTEN BACKED WITH BLACK VELVET OR MIRRORS.

·AURICULA·

AURICULA

FLOWERS COME IN MANY COLOURS, SOME WITH FROSTING (KNOWN
AS FARINA OR MEAL). LIKE OTHER ALPINES, THEY NEED GOOD
DRAINAGE AND GROW WELL IN A COLD FRAME OR GREENHOUSE.

PRIMULAS HAVE BEEN GROWN IN COTTAGE GARDENS SINCE TUDOR
TIMES. PRIMROSES HAVE LOTS OF STEMS DISPLAYING A SINGLE
FLOWER. POLYANTHAS BEAR LOTS OF FLOWERS ON A SINGLE STEM.
PRIMULAS COME IN A RANGE OF WONDERFUL COLOURS AND LOVE
A HUMUS-RICH SOIL WITH GENEROUS AMOUNTS OF LEAF MOULD
AND COMPOST. DIVIDE CLUMPS EVERY FEW YEARS AFTER THEY
HAVE FINISHED FLOWERING. THE FLOWERS CRYSTALLISE WELL,
AND ARE LOVELY FOR DECORATING PUDDINGS AND CAKES.~

AQUILEGIA

AQUILEGIA, GROWN IN BRITAIN SINCE THE 16TH CENTURY, IS ALSO CALLED GRANNY'S BONNET & COLUMBINE (FROM COLUMBA – A DOVE, THE PETALS RESEMBLING THE FLYING BIRD). MOST AQUILEGIA HAVE FIVE SPURS AND WILL GROW IN WELL-DRAINED SOIL IN SUN OR PARTIAL SHADE. THEY SELF-SEED VERY HAPPILY, THEIR PROMISCUITY RESULTING IN MANY INTERESTING OFFSPRING. ONE OF THE MOST ADMIRED AQUILEGIA IS A. VULGARIS 'NORA BARLOW' NAMED AFTER CHARLES DARWIN'S GRANDDAUGHTER, IN WHOSE GARDEN IT GREW FOR MANY YEARS. IT IS ONE OF THE FEW AQUILEGIA THAT COMES TRUE FROM SEED. ALTHOUGH WILLIAM TURNER RECOMMENDED IN 1568 "IF DRUNK WITH WINE IT IS GOOD FOR JAUNDICE," THE PLANT IS POISONOUS. "VERY COMMON, BUT VERY PRETTY." 1819
W. COBBETT

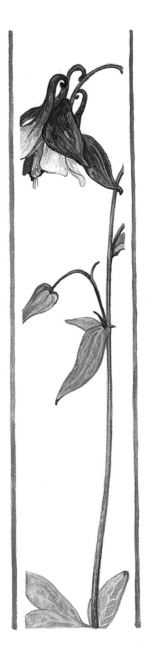

Aquilegia vulgaris

NORA BARLOW

Bring hither the pink and purple columbine, With gilliflowers:

E. Spenser 1579

SPRING FLOWERS

AUBRIETA · An evergreen perennial that thrives in limey soils. Cut back after flowering to encourage more flowers.

JAPANESE QUINCE (CHAENOMELES) · This hardy plant is excellent grown against a wall. Prune it after flowering.

ALYSSUM · Loved by butterflies and bees, it is ideal for sunny walls and banks. Cut it back hard after flowering.

PULMONARIA · A tough plant that thrives in sun or partial shade. The pink flowers turn to blue as they mature.

SAXIFRAGE · Sprays of dainty pink flowers are borne above a cushion of small leaves. Ideal for edging paths.

BERGENIA · Also known as Elephant's Ears, this evergreen makes an excellent ground cover. It flowers best in full sun.

PERIWINKLE (VINCA) · Good for ground cover in shady or dry places. The flowers come in various shades of blue.

BLEEDING HEART (DICENTRA) · A tall plant flowering best in semi-shade. The foliage dies down in the summer.

CORYDALIS FLEXUOSA · This perennial plant with pretty lacey foliage thrives in sun and also partial shade.

BELLIS · This daisy with its long flowering period has been grown for many years. Divide in spring or autumn.

ARABIS · Cheerfully tumbling over low walls, arabis grows in any well-drained soil. Dead head after flowering.

AUBRIETA

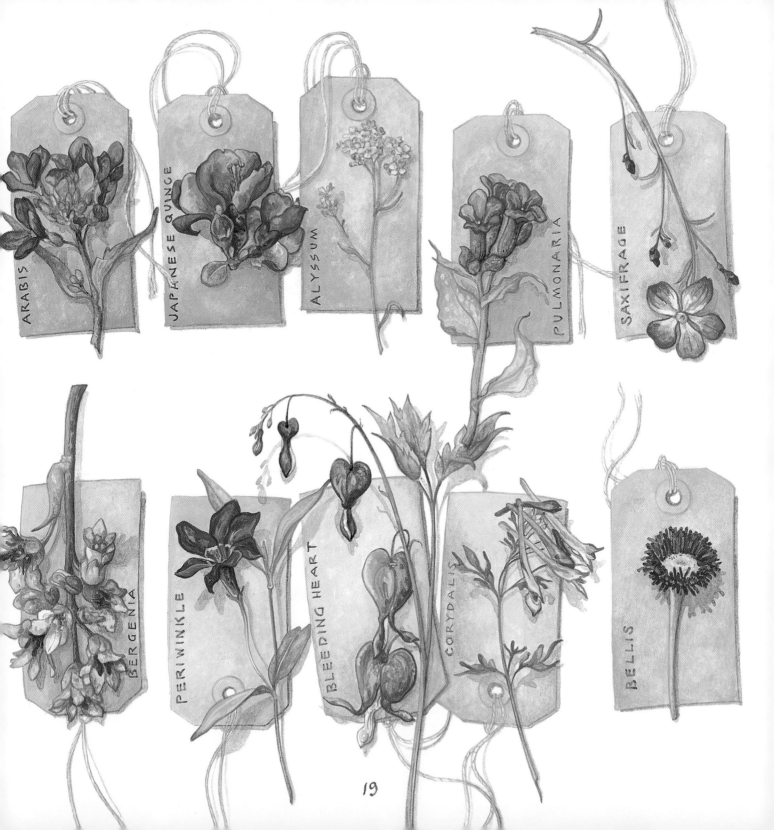

ARABIS

JAPANESE QUINCE

ALYSSUM

PULMONARIA

SAXIFRAGE

BERGENIA

PERIWINKLE

BLEEDING HEART

CORYDALIS

BELLIS

19

LOVED SINCE CLASSICAL TIMES, VIOLETS WERE NOT
BROUGHT INTO THE HOUSE BY COUNTRY PEOPLE FOR
FEAR OF INTRODUCING FLEAS. "THAT WHICH ABOVE
ALL OTHERS YIELDS THE SWEETEST SMELL IN
THE AIR IS THE VIOLET." FRANCIS BACON 1612

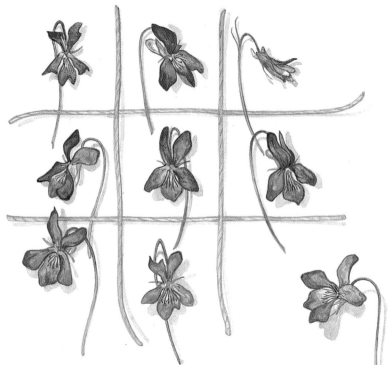

VIOLA ODORATA IS HAPPY GROWING IN SUN OR SHADE.
IT BLOOMS IN THE SPRING AND SPREADS EASILY BY
RUNNERS OR BY SELF SEEDING. SINCE MEDIEVAL
TIMES THE FLOWERS HAVE BEEN USED TO DECORATE
SALADS AND FOR CRYSTALLISING. LEAF MOULD
KEEPS THE SOIL MOIST AROUND THE PLANTS.

CRYSTALLISED

FLOWERS

Edible flowers crystallise well & are
lovely on cakes and puddings. Brush egg
white, which has been lightly beaten, onto
each flower. Dip in caster sugar and leave
to dry in a warm place before using. Edible
flowers include primroses, pansies, borage,
rose petals, pinks and marigold petals.

· WHEN & HOW TO SOW VEGETABLE SEEDS ·

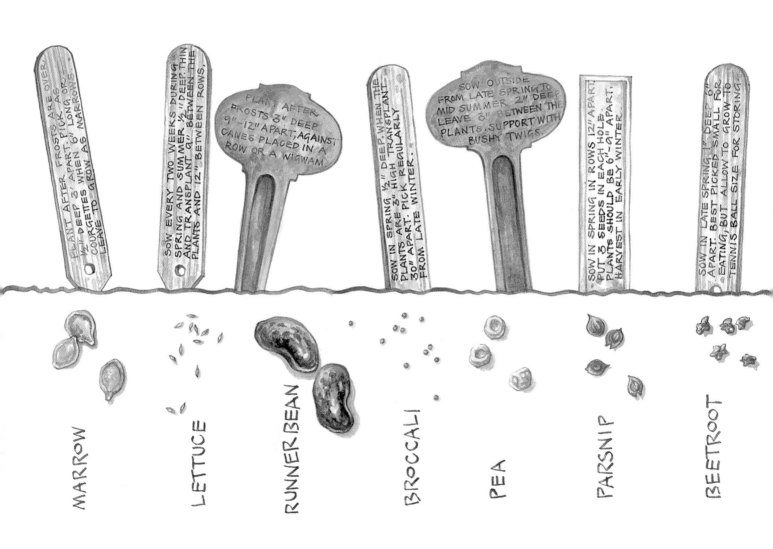

PLANT AFTER FROSTS ARE OVER. ½" DEEP 3' APART. PICK AS COURGETTES WHEN 6" LONG OR LEAVE TO GROW AS MARROWS.

SOW EVERY TWO WEEKS DURING SPRING AND SUMMER ½" DEEP. THIN AND TRANSPLANT 9". BETWEEN THE PLANTS AND 12" BETWEEN ROWS.

PLANT AFTER FROSTS 3" DEEP 9"-12" APART, AGAINST CANES PLACED IN A ROW OR A WIGWAM.

SOW IN SPRING ½" DEEP. WHEN THE PLANTS ARE 3" HIGH TRANSPLANT 30" APART. PICK REGULARLY FROM LATE WINTER.

SOW OUTSIDE FROM LATE SPRING TO MID SUMMER 2" DEEP LEAVE 3" BETWEEN THE PLANTS. SUPPORT WITH BUSHY TWIGS.

SOW IN SPRING IN ROWS 12" APART. PUT 3 SEEDS IN EACH HOLE. PLANTS SHOULD BE 6"-9" APART. HARVEST IN EARLY WINTER.

SOW IN LATE SPRING 1" DEEP 6" APART. BEST PICKED SMALL FOR EATING, BUT ALLOW TO GROW TO TENNIS BALL SIZE FOR STORING.

MARROW

LETTUCE

RUNNER BEAN

BROCCALI

PEA

PARSNIP

BEETROOT

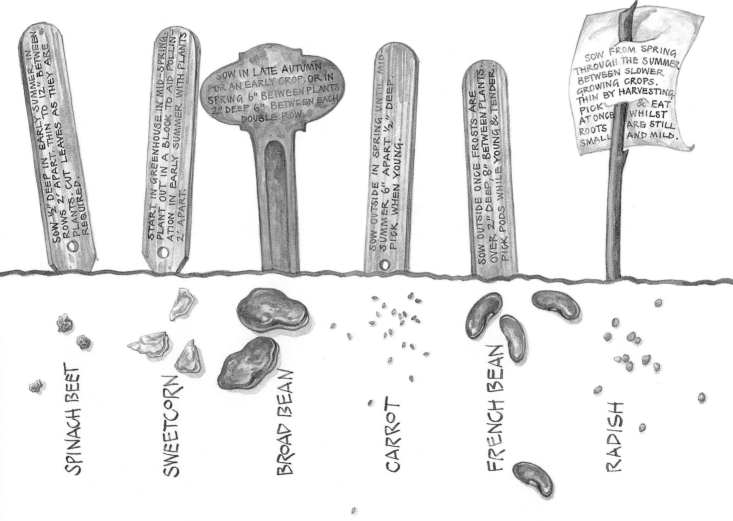

SOW ½" DEEP IN EARLY SUMMER IN ROWS 2' APART. THIN TO 12" BETWEEN PLANTS. CUT LEAVES AS THEY ARE REQUIRED.

START IN GREENHOUSE IN MID-SPRING. PLANT OUT IN A BLOCK TO AID POLLIN- ATION IN EARLY SUMMER WITH PLANTS 2' APART.

SOW IN LATE AUTUMN FOR AN EARLY CROP, OR IN SPRING 6" BETWEEN PLANTS 2" DEEP 6" BETWEEN EACH DOUBLE ROW.

SOW OUTSIDE IN SPRING UNTIL MID- SUMMER 6" APART ½" DEEP. PICK WHEN YOUNG.

SOW OUTSIDE ONCE FROSTS ARE OVER. 2" DEEP, 8" BETWEEN PLANTS. PICK PODS WHILE YOUNG & TENDER.

SOW FROM SPRING THROUGH THE SUMMER BETWEEN SLOWER GROWING CROPS. THIN BY HARVESTING. PICK & EAT AT ONCE WHILST ROOTS ARE STILL SMALL AND MILD.

SPINACH BEET

SWEETCORN

BROAD BEAN

CARROT

FRENCH BEAN

RADISH

ALL MEASUREMENTS ARE IN INCHES AND ARE APPROXIMATE

PLANT FOUR SEEDS IN A ROW
ONE FOR THE MOUSE AND ONE FOR THE CROW
ONE TO ROT AND ONE TO GROW

SOW PEASEN AND BEANS IN THE WANE OF THE MOON

WHO SOWETH THEM SOONER HE SOWETH TOO SOON
Thomas Tusser

PERENNIAL WEEDS ARE DIFFICULT TO GET RID OF. DIG OUT AS MUCH ROOT AS POSSIBLE. DO NOT ADD TO COMPOST HEAP BUT THROW THEM AWAY.

GROUND ELDER WAS USED TO TREAT GOUT IN THE MIDDLE AGES. FOUND IN MONASTERY GARDENS IT WAS CALLED BISHOPS WEED. DIG OUT THE INVASIVE ROOTS. PLANT MARIGOLDS TO DETER SPREADING.

EARLY AMERICAN SETTLERS INTRODUCED MANY ENGLISH WEEDS TO AMERICA SUCH AS COUCH GRASS, DANDELION, CHICKWEED AND NETTLE.

DOCK LEAVES HAVE BEEN USED FOR MANY YEARS TO RUB ON NETTLE STINGS. DIG OUT THE ROOTS BEFORE THEY SEED & SPREAD. "THEIR ROOTS GO DEEPER THAN CONSCIENCE." C. DUDLEY WARNER 1871

PERENNIAL WEEDS ○ PERENNIAL WEEDS ○ PERENNIAL WEED

·GROUND ELDER· ·BINDWEED· ·COUCH GRASS· ·HORSETAIL· ·DOCK· ·BUTTERCUP·

PERENNIAL WEEDS ○ PERENNIAL WEEDS ○ PERENNIAL WEED

COUCH GRASS IS VERY INVASIVE AND EVERY PIECE OF ROOT MUST BE REMOVED. SOW TURNIP SEED THICKLY IN IT TO CLEAR THE GROUND.

BINDWEED, A PURGATIVE, WAS ALSO CALLED DEVIL'S GUTS. IT QUICKLY SMOTHERS OTHER PLANTS SO DIG OUT EVERY LAST BIT OF ROOT.

HORSETAIL OR MARESTAIL, IS SO CALLED FROM ITS BUSHY APPEARANCE. USED TO SCOUR AND POLISH PEWTER, IT HAS GROWN SINCE PREHISTORIC TIMES.

BUTTERCUPS SPREAD BY SEEDING & BY CREEPING RUNNERS. ENJOY THIS WILD FLOWER BY PICKING A LARGE BUNCH FOR THE KITCHEN TABLE.

HAND WEEDING OR HOEING REGULARLY IS THE MOST EFFECTIVE MEANS OF CONTROL. TRY TO WEED BEFORE THE WEEDS FLOWER AND SEED.

• • •

CLEAVERS, ALSO CALLED GOOSEGRASS, WAS ONCE USED TO CURDLE MILK. THE STICKY STEMS & SEEDS GIVE IT NAMES SUCH AS BURWEED, STICKLEBACK, CATCHGRASS & STICKY WILLY.

GROUNDSEL IS ATTRACTIVE TO BUTTERFLIES AND BEES, AS WELL AS PET RABBITS & POULTRY. ITS SHALLOW ROOTS MAKE IT EASY TO PULL UP.

• • •

FAT HEN WAS EATEN IN THE MIDDLE AGES AS A VEGETABLE, LIKE SPINACH, AND ALSO BY IRON AGE PEOPLE. ITS TINY GREEN FLOWERS ATTRACT BEES AND ALSO HOVERFLIES WHICH EAT UP APHIDS.

ANNUAL WEEDS • ANNUAL WEEDS • ANNUAL WEEDS

• CHICKWEED • GROUNDSEL • HERB ROBERT • FAT HEN •

ANNUAL WEEDS • ANNUAL WEEDS • ANNUAL WEEDS

HERB ROBERT, OR STINKING BOB BECAUSE OF ITS PUNGENT SMELL, IS A MEMBER OF THE CRANESBILL FAMILY. IT IS PRETTY ENOUGH TO KEEP A LITTLE OF.

• • •

"WEEDS ARE THE LITTLE VICES THAT BESET PLANT LIFE, & ARE TO BE GOT RID OF THE BEST WAY WE KNOW HOW." FARMERS ALMANAC 1881

CHICKWEED, DESPITE ITS STRAGGLY APPEARANCE, GROWS STRONGLY MOST OF THE YEAR. IT CAN BE EATEN BOTH RAW & COOKED. BIRDS LIKE ITS SEEDS.

• • •

"DO NOT BE AFRAID OF WEEDS, BUT CUT AWAY. THEY MUST EITHER BE YOUR MASTER OR YOU THEIRS." EVERYMAN HIS OWN GARDENER. 1845.

27

"Magicians say that if
a person rub himself
all over with it, he will
everywhere be welcome
and obtain what he
wishes." MATTHIOLUS 1565

∘ D A N D E L I O N ∘

The name dandelion is derived from the French dents de lion-a reference to its serrated leaves. If you cannot rid your garden of it, feed it to your rabbits or eat it. The young leaves are good in salads. Dandelion wine is delicious, and the roasted roots are used as a coffee substitute. A diuretic, it was called pis-a-bed.

"A well-known & most wicked garden weed, in this country as well as England. In the spring (1817) when I came to Long Island & when nothing in the shape of greens was to be had for love or money, Dandelions were our resource, and I have always since that time looked at this weed with a more friendly eye." W. Cobbett
THE AMERICAN GARDENER

These little flowers bespangle the lawns and the meadows. W. Cobbett 1813

"The juice of the leaves and roots snift up into the nosthrils, purgeth the head mightily, and helpeth the megrim. The same given to little dogs with milke, keepeth them from growing great." GERARD 1597

The stinging nettle provides an important food source for butterfly caterpillars, so leave some in a corner of the garden. When the leaves are left to soak in a barrel of water for 3 weeks, the resultant liquid makes a highly nutritious feed for plants. Like comfrey, if added to the compost heap, it will help speed up decomposition. To rid your garden of any unwanted nettles, dig them out.

NE
PRO
EXC
PER

NETTLE PLA
FERTILE GRO
RUB DOCK LEA
THE FIBROUS ROO   ED TO MAKE TWINE.
"COTTAGERS NOW GATHER THE TENDER-SPRINGING
TOPS OF NETTLES TO MAKE POTTAGE, CONSIDERED
BY THEM A GREAT PURIFIER OF THE BLOOD." W.
HOWITT 1833; – A BELIEF WHICH IS STILL HELD BY
SOME TODAY. PICK THE YOUNG TOPS IN SPRING,
BEFORE THE NETTLE FLOWERS, TO MAKE SOUP.

LEAF

CORNUS   HOSTA   PRIMROSE

FATSIA   IRIS   FERN

VEINS

·LEAF PROBLEMS·

·MAGNESIUM DEFICIENCY·
FEED WITH SEAWEED.

·VIRUS·
NO CURE SO THROW AWAY INFECTED PLANT. DO NOT PUT ON COMPOST
HEAP.

·SNAIL AND SLUG DAMAGE·
SURROUND VULNERABLE PLANTS WITH GRAVEL, SAWDUST, LIME,
SOOT, SHARP SAND OR HOLLY LEAVES. CATCH IN SAUCERS OF BEER OR
INVERTED ORANGE SKINS. ENCOURAGE BIRDS, FROGS AND HEDGEHOGS
INTO THE GARDEN TO EAT SLUGS AND SNAILS.

·MILDEW·
SPRAY WITH AN INFUSION OF HORSETAIL. BURN INFECTED LEAVES. AVOID
OVER-WATERING AND INCREASE AIR FLOW ROUND PLANTS BY NOT PLANTING
TOO CLOSE TOGETHER.

·VINE WEEVIL DAMAGE·
DESTROY BEETLES ON SIGHT. CHECK ROOT BALL OF NEW PLANTS FOR ANY
GRUBS. CONTROL WITH PARASITIC NEMATODES.

·LEAF SPOT·
BURN AFFECTED LEAVES. GROW CHIVES NEAR ROSES TO PREVENT THIS.

·LEAF CUTTING BEE·
THE FEMALE BEE CUTS PIECES OF LEAF TO LINE HER NEST. LITTLE DAMAGE
IS CAUSED TO THE PLANT.

·RUST·
BURN AFFECTED LEAVES. APPLY POTASH.

·POTASSIUM DEFICIENCY·
APPLY POTASH AND ORGANIC FERTILISER.

PREVENT MANY DISEASES BY KEEPING PLANTS HEALTHY WITH ORGANIC FERTILIZER AND GOOD
GARDEN HYGIENE.

Vine weevil

·MAGNESIUM DEFICIENCY.

·SNAIL DAMAGE.

·VINE WEEVIL DAMAGE.

·VIRUS.

·MILDEW.

·LEAF PROBLEMS·

·LEAF MINER·

·RUST·

·LEAF SPOT·

·LEAF-CUTTING BEE·

·POTASSIUM DEFICIENCY·

35

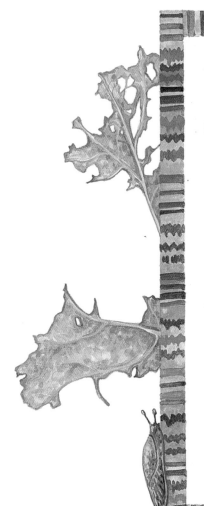

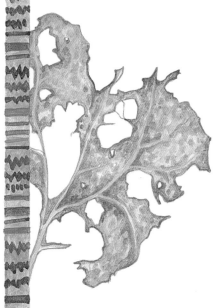

SLUGS AND SNAILS CAN CAUSE A LOT OF DAMAGE TO PLANTS IN THE GARDEN. SURROUND VULNERABLE PLANTS WITH SOOT, LIME, WOODASH, PINE NEEDLES, SAWDUST, PRICKLY HOLLY LEAVES, GRAVEL OR CRUSHED EGG SHELLS. CATCH SLUGS AND SNAILS IN INVERTED GRAPEFRUIT SKINS, CABBAGE LEAVES AND SUNKEN SAUCERS OF BEER. ENCOURAGE BIRDS, HEDGEHOGS AND FROGS INTO THE GARDEN TO EAT THESE PESTS. GO OUT AT NIGHT AND PICK SLUGS & SNAILS OFF PLANTS WHEN THEY ARE FEEDING. SNAILS CAN LIVE FOR UP TO THREE YEARS, THEIR SHELLS GETTING BIGGER AS THEY GROW. "EVEN A CREATURE SO HUMBLE AND SO DESPICABLE AS A SLUG, IS AS CURIOUSLY & WONDERFULLY MADE...AS THE NOBLEST & MOST BEAUTIFUL ANIMAL". J. LOUDON 1845

36

POP EMPTY SNAIL SHELLS ON
GARDEN CANES TO PROTECT
EYES FROM INJURY.

The snail "is very
mischievous amongst
the plants in the
garden in general:
... In winter time,
in dry and frosty
weather, snails
should be routed
out from all their
fastnesses, and
destroyed. This is
the most effectual
way of guarding
against their de-
precations; for,
when the leaves
come out, they have
shelter, they are
exceedingly cunning
in availing them-
selves of that ~
shelter; but though
you finally discover
& kill them, they
spoil your fruit first."
WILLIAM COBBETT 1829

The Siberian iris is the easiest iris to grow, and produces masses of flowers in the early summer. It grows in sun or partial shade. Split clumps in autumn or spring. The iris is depicted in the Egyptian temple at Karnak. "I know of no flower that better repays the time & attention of the horticulturist." 1819

W. MASTERS

· iris sibirica ·

Bearded iris come in a vast range of colours.
An iris with a tuft of hairs on the down-
ward arching petal called the fall is a ~
bearded iris. Irises must be planted in a
sunny spot with good drainage where the
rhizomes can be baked by the sun. Iris
germanica should be divided every few years.

·bearded iris·

PANSIES COME IN A WIDE RANGE OF GLORIOUS
COLOURS ~ PURPLE, BLUE, LAVENDER, VIOLET,
RED, PINK, PLUM, WINE RED, YELLOW, CREAM,
WHITE, BRONZE, RUST AND APRICOT AND MORE.

PANSIES PREFER A WELL~DRAINED & SUNNY
POSITION AND ARE BEST GROWN AS AN ANNUAL
OR BIENNIAL, BRINGING A WELCOME SPLASH
OF COLOUR TO BORDERS, TUBS AND HANGING
BASKETS.

DEAD HEAD REGULARLY TO ENCOURAGE MORE
BLOOMS. CUT THE PLANTS BACK WHEN THEY
BECOME LEGGY, FEED, AND THEY WILL SOON
FLOWER AGAIN. INCREASE BY CUTTINGS TAKEN
IN LATE SUMMER, OR BY DIVISION.

PANSIES ARE EDIBLE SO FREEZE THEM IN ICE
CUBES, FLOAT THEM IN SUMMER DRINKS, &
USE THEM TO DECORATE CAKES.

THE LARGE SHOWY BLOOMS OF THE PANSY WERE DEVELOPED IN THE 1830'S. BY 1840 THERE WERE 400 NAMED VARIETIES. PANSIES WERE CULTIVATED FROM THE TINY VIOLA TRICOLOR, ALSO CALLED KISS- ME-QUICK, HEARTSEASE, JOHNNY-JUMP-UP, CUPID'S FLOWER, TICKLE-MY-FANCY AND MANY MORE.

THE PANSY WAS USED IN LOVE POTIONS AND IS ASSOCIATED WITH ST. VALENTINE'S DAY. PANSY LEAVES WERE SAID TO MEND A BROKEN HEART. TO DREAM OF PANSIES PROMISES CONTENTMENT. "THERE'S ROSEMARY, THAT'S FOR REMEMBRANCE; PRAY, LOVE, REMEMBER: AND THERE IS PANSIES, THAT'S FOR THOUGHTS" Shakespeare 1601

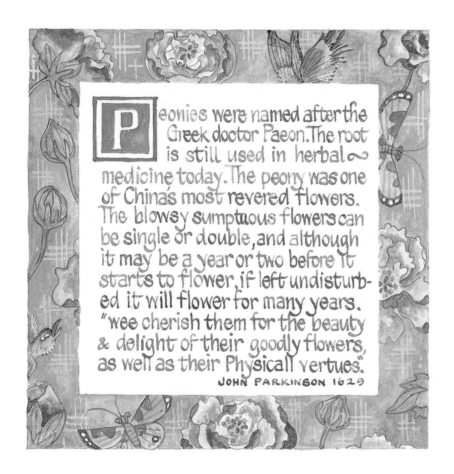

Peonies were named after the Greek doctor Paeon. The root is still used in herbal medicine today. The peony was one of China's most revered flowers. The blowsy sumptuous flowers can be single or double, and although it may be a year or two before it starts to flower, if left undisturbed it will flower for many years. "wee cherish them for the beauty & delight of their goodly flowers, as well as their Physicall vertues."

JOHN PARKINSON 1629

COLOUR IN THE GARDEN

DESIGNER GOUACHE BLUE 14ml e

sky   violet   Prussian   Cobalt   Ultramarine

DECKCHAIR CANVAS

cadmium   plum   magenta   rose   crimson

DESIGNER GOUACHE RED 14ml e

ANNUALS
FOIL PACKED
Petunia
STAR SERIES   45 seeds

cushion fabric

lemon   yellow ochre   raw sienna   cowslip   cadmium

DESIGNER GOUACHE YELLOW 14ml e

...able ...high ...style ...rden.

COLOUR IN THE GARDEN

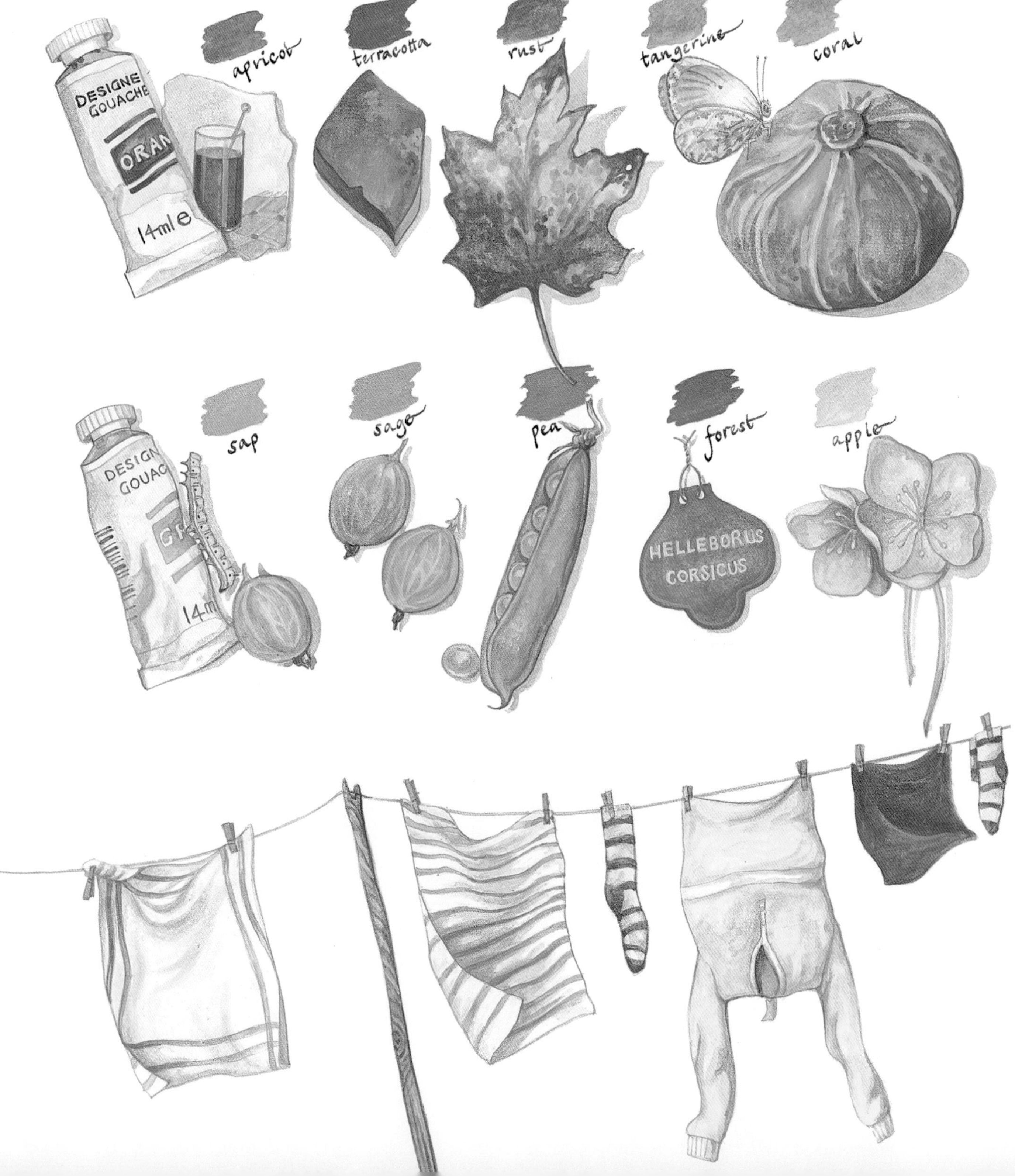
DESIGNE
GOUACHE
ORAN
14ml e
apricot
terracotta
rust
tangerine
coral
DESIGN
GOUAC
14ml
sap
sage
pea
forest
apple
HELLEBORUS
CORSICUS

SUMMER

THE SUMMER'S FLOWER IS TO THE SUMMER SWEET

SHAKESPEARE

·SEASONAL TASKS·

- TAKE CUTTINGS OF SHRUBS AND CLIMBERS
- SOW ANNUALS IN SITU
- PLANT OUT TENDER BEDDING PLANTS ONCE DANGER OF FROST IS OVER
- DEADHEAD ROSES AND PERENNIALS TO ENCOURAGE FURTHER FLOWERS
- CUT FLOWERS AND SEEDHEADS AND HERBS FOR DRYING
- WATER NEWLY PLANTED PLANTS AND CONTAINERS WELL
- KEEP WEEDING
- TIE IN CLIMBERS
- PLANT AUTUMN FLOWERING BULBS
- TRIM FAST GROWING HEDGES REGULARLY
- EARTH UP POTATOES
- DIVIDE IRISES
- PLANT UP TUBS AND WINDOWBOXES
- CONTINUE SUCCESSIONAL SOWING OF LETTUCE AND CARROTS

·SUMMER·

IF YOU WANT TO BE HAPPY FOR A LIFETIME PLANT A GARDEN

I have a garden   of my own

shining with flowers   of every hue

I loved it dearly   while alone

but I shall love it   more with You.

THOMAS MORE 1836

49

Geranium macrorrhizum

Tulipa 'Queen of Night'

Helleborus orientalis

Camellia 'Inspiration'

Chaenomeles 'Nicoline'

Lychnis coronaria

Rosa 'The Fairy'

Paeonia veitchii

Penstemon 'Garnet'

Astrantia major

Cosmos 'Sensation'

Anemone hupehensis

Salvia involucrata

Schizostylis coccinea

Sedum spectabile

Nerine bowdenii

· SPRING ·

Tulipa 'Angelique'

Lamium maculatum

Saxifraga geum

Oxalis adenophylla

Dicentra spectabilis

· SUMMER ·

Rosa 'Roseraie de l'Hay'

Geranium psilostemon

Papaver orientale 'Allegro Viva'

Kalmia latifolia

Polygonum bistorta 'Superbum'

Sidalcea 'Jimmy Whittet'

· AUTUMN ·

Colchicum bivonae

Dahlia 'Bishop of Llandaff'

Eupatorium purpureum

Aster novae-angliae

Phlox paniculata

· GERANIUM ·

· ROSA GLAUCA ·

· KNAUTIA ·

SWEET WILLIAM

· NEMESIA ·

· FUCHSIA ·

· JAPANESE ANEMONE ·

· PENSTEMON ·

· CISTUS ·

· POLYGONUM ·

· SIDALCEA ·

· LYCHNIS ·

· BEGONIA ·

· THRIFT ·

· PHUOPSIS ·

· FRAGARIA ·

· PELARGONIUM ·

· BUSY LIZZIE ·

· GERANIUM ·

Tulipa 'Apricot Beauty'
Potentilla fruiticosa 'Daydawn'
Fritillaria imperialis
Euphorbia polychroma
Crocus 'E.A.Bowles'

Ligularia przewalskii
Cephalaria gigantea
Rosa 'Graham Thomas'
Thunbergia alata
Achillea 'Coronation Gold'
Coreopsis lanceolata

Helenium 'Wyndley'
Crocosmia 'Jackanapes'
Helianthus 'Loddon Gold'
Chrysanthemum 'Autumn Days'
Helenium 'Moerheim Beauty'

· SPRING ·

Doronicum orientale
Rosa 'Canary Bird'
Crocus 'Cream Beauty'
Narcissus 'Golden Ducat'
Meconopsis cambrica

· SUMMER ·

Verbascum 'Gainsborough'
Heliopsis 'Ballet Dancer'
Geum borisii
Alstroemeria aurea
Phlomis fruiticosa
Rosa 'Golden Showers'

· AUTUMN ·

Tropaeolum tuberosum
Kniphofia 'Percy's Pride'
Dahlia 'Butterball'
Helianthus annus
Rudbeckia 'Herbstsonne'

·JASMINE·

·ESCHSCHOLZIA·

·HYPERICUM·

·LIMNANTHES·

·COREOPSIS·

·FEVERFEW·

·GEUM·

·HONEYSUCKLE·

·LYSIMACHIA·

·BRIMSTONE
BUTTERFLY·

·SENECIO·

·ROSA GOLDFINCH·

·ROCK ROSE·

·SISYRINCHIUM·

·MARIGOLD·

·POTENTILLA·

·NASTURTIUM·

·ALLIUM·

·CORONILLA·

·ANTHEMIS·

- Meconopsis betonicifolia
- Camassia leichtlinii
- Lathyrus vernus
- Veronica gentianoides
- Omphalodes cappadocica

- Campanula glomerata 'Superba'
- Echinops ritro 'Veitch's Blue'
- Anchusa azurea 'Loddon Royalist'
- Linum narbonense
- Tradescantia 'Purple Dome'
- Geranium 'Johnson's Blue'

- Aster frikartii 'Mönch'
- Verbena bonariensis
- Aconitum 'Newry Blue'
- Caryopteris
- Liriope muscari

·SPRING·

- Chionodoxa
- Gentiana verna
- Clematis alpina 'Frances Rivis'
- Syringa persica
- Muscari armeniacum

·SUMMER·

- Salvia patens
- Stachys macrantha
- Scabiosa caucasia
- Clematis 'Jackmanii'
- Phlox 'Chatahoochee'
- Eryngium oliverianum

·AUTUMN·

- Ceratostigma willmottianum
- Clematis viticella 'Etoile Violette'
- Aster novi-belgii 'Marie Bellard'
- Agapanthus orientalis
- Cerinthe major 'Purpurascens'

56

VIOLA

FORGET ME NOT

CRANESBILL

PERIWINKLE

VIOLA

BRUNNERA

PRIMULA

PULMONARIA

VIOLA

POLEMONIUM

AQUILEGIA

FRENCH LAVENDER

CORNFLOWER

ANCHUSA

AUBRETIA

AUBRETIA

AJUGA

ERYSIMUM

ROSES

Gather ye rosebuds
while ye may,
Old Time is still
a flying:
And this same flower
that smiles today,
To-morrow will be
dying.

Herrick 1648

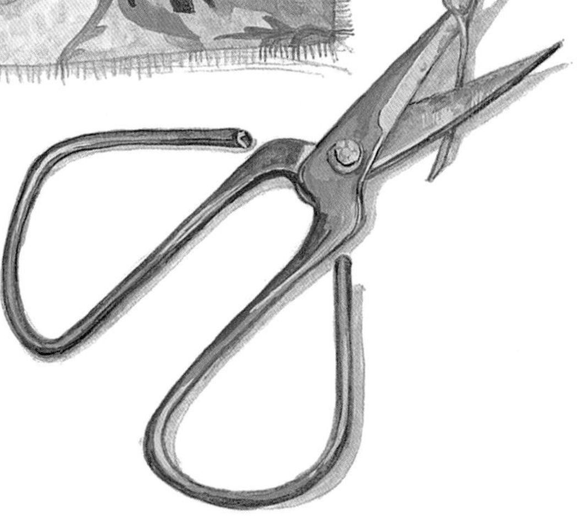

EGYPTIAN ROSES WERE
WHEN THE ITALIAN ROSES
NERO'S ORDER MILLIONS
STREWN IN THE STREETS
EMPRESS JOSEPHINE
ROSE GARDENS AT MAL-
WERE PLANTED ENTIRELY
REDOUTÉ PAINTED THEM
DUE TO THEIR POPULARITY,
1,393 VARIETIES IN STOCK.
WERE A GREAT FAVOURITE
TEA ROSES WERE NAMED AFTER
OF CHINA TEA FROM THEIR
NEXT TO A ROSE BUSH WILL
SPOONFUL OF SUGAR IN THE
ROSES LIVE LONGER. THE
OVER 60 TIMES BY WILLIAM
I HAVE PLUCK'D THY ROSE, I
VITAL GROWTH AGAIN, IT NEEDS
SMELL IT ON THE TREE." 1602.
DESERVE THE CHIEFEST AND
AMONG ALL FLOWERS WHATSO-
ESTEEMED FOR HIS BEAUTIE,

SHIPPED TO ROME
WERE OUT OF BLOOM. ON
OF ROSE PETALS WERE
DURING FESTIVALS. THE
CREATED ONE OF THE FIRST
MAISON WHERE MANY BEDS
WITH ROSES. THE ARTIST
AT HER REQUEST. BY 1826,
A LONDON NURSERY HAD
ROSE PETAL SANDWICHES
AT VICTORIAN TEA PARTIES.
THE DELICATE FRAGRANCE
PETALS. GARLIC BURIED
DETER GREENFLY. A
WATER WILL HELP CUT
ROSE IS MENTIONED
SHAKESPEARE."WHEN
CANNOT GIVE IT
MUST WITHER: I'LL
" THE ROSE DOTH
MOST PRINCIPAL PLACE
EVER, BEING NOT ONLY
VERTUES, AND HIS

FRAGRANT & ODORIFEROUS SMELL; BUT ALSO BECAUSE IT IS
THE HONOUR & ORNAMENT OF OUR ENGLISH SCEPTER." GERARD
1545

·NEVADA·

·GERTRUDE JEKYLL·

·NATALIE NYPELS·

·PINK PERPETUE·

·WILLIAM LOBB·

·MAIGOLD·

·LEONTINE GERVAIS·

·ROSA MUNDI·

·FRENCHAM·

·TUSCANY·

·BONICA·

·PENELOPE·

Take drie Rose
leaves, keep them close in a
glasse which will keep them sweet,
then take powder of Mints, powder
of Cloves in a grosse powder. Put the
same to the Rose leaves then put
all these together in a bag, and
take that to bed with you, and it
will cause you to sleep, and it is
good to smell unto at other times.
Ram's Little Dodoen 1606

Roses should not be planted in ground where roses have previously grown or they will not thrive. They prefer a sunny position with fertile soil.

Hybrid tea and floribunda roses need to be pruned to stimulate vigorous growth. Old fashioned shrub roses need little attention. To prune cut out dead wood and spindly growth. Cut stems to about 10" (25 cms.), cutting just above an outward facing bud. Prune roses in the spring. Feed and mulch after pruning.

Rose bushes in windy exposed areas can be lightly pruned in the autumn to help prevent possible damage.

Prune climbing roses in the autumn, cutting back sideshoots to 6" (15 cms.) from the main stem. Tie in any new stems.

Dead head roses to encourage more flowers. Some roses, like rosa glauca, should not have dead flowers removed or they will not bear their beautiful hips.

A clove of garlic planted next to a rose bush will deter aphids, as will chives & parsley. Garlic also protects against mildew & black-spot. Buried banana skins provide roses with potash.

O, my Luve's like
a red red rose —
That's newly sprung
in June —
R. Burns
1796

RED RED ROSES • DUBLIN BAY • FIRE PRINCESS • DORTMUND

ALEC'S RED • FRAU DAGMAR HASTRUP • PRECIOUS PLATINUM • ALEXANDER

SCARLET FIRE • ROSERAIE DE L'HAY • WEE JOCK • GUINÉE

RED ACE • ROYAL WILLIAM • ROSA MOYESII • GERANIUM • DANSE DU FEU

·VERBASCUM·
Mullein

These herbaceous
perennials or
biennials prefer
full sun and well
drained soil. Some
of the mulleins
self-seed freely
& look particularly
good growing in
gravel. 3'-5' high.

64

· A COLLECTION OF TALL PLANTS FOR SUMMER BORDERS ·

HOLLYHOCK ANGELICA FOXGLOVE DELPHINIUM SUNFLOWER

SOME THINK THE 'HOLY HOC' WAS BROUGHT OVER FROM PALESTINE BY CRUSADERS. BEE STINGS WERE TREATED WITH A POULTICE OF THE LEAVES.' HOLLIHOCK RISETH HIGH; SEEDETH AND DYETH '. W. Lawson 1617

THE CANDIED STEM WAS THOUGHT GOOD FOR 'WIND AND STRENGTHENING THE STOMACH' 'THE ROOT OF GARDEN ANGELICA IS A SINGULAR REMEDY AGAINST POYSON AND AGAINST THE PLAGUE'. Gerard 1597

IT WAS THOUGHT THE FAIRIES GAVE THE FLOWERS TO THE FOXES TO PUT ON THEIR PAWS SO THEY COULD SNEAK UP QUIETLY ON THEIR PREY. ALSO KNOWN AS DEAD MAN'S BELLS BECAUSE IT IS POISONOUS.

GETS ITS NAME FROM THE GREEK NAME FOR DOLPHIN AS THE FLOWERS RESEMBLE A DOLPHIN'S NOSE. A SOLUTION MADE FROM THE SEEDS WILL KILL HEAD LICE. THE PLANT IS POISONOUS.

ORIGINALLY FROM SOUTH AMERICA. DEPICTIONS OF IT HAVE BEEN FOUND IN INCA TEMPLES. 'FIT FOR NOTHING BUT VERY EXTENSIVE SHRUBBERIES. WHEN SEEN FROM A DISTANCE, THE SIGHT MAY ENDURE IT.' W Cobbett 1833

DIANTHUS.

Pinks and carnations need a sunny spot and well drained soil.
Ideal for edging paths, many are scented, like Mrs Sinkins (so
called after the wife of the Master of Slough Workhouse) & are
excellent for cutting. Cottage pinks flower prolifically all summer
whilst modern pinks are repeat flowering. Border carnations may
need staking. Replace plants every few years, taking side shoot
or heel cuttings in the summer, & plant up in pots of sandy soil.

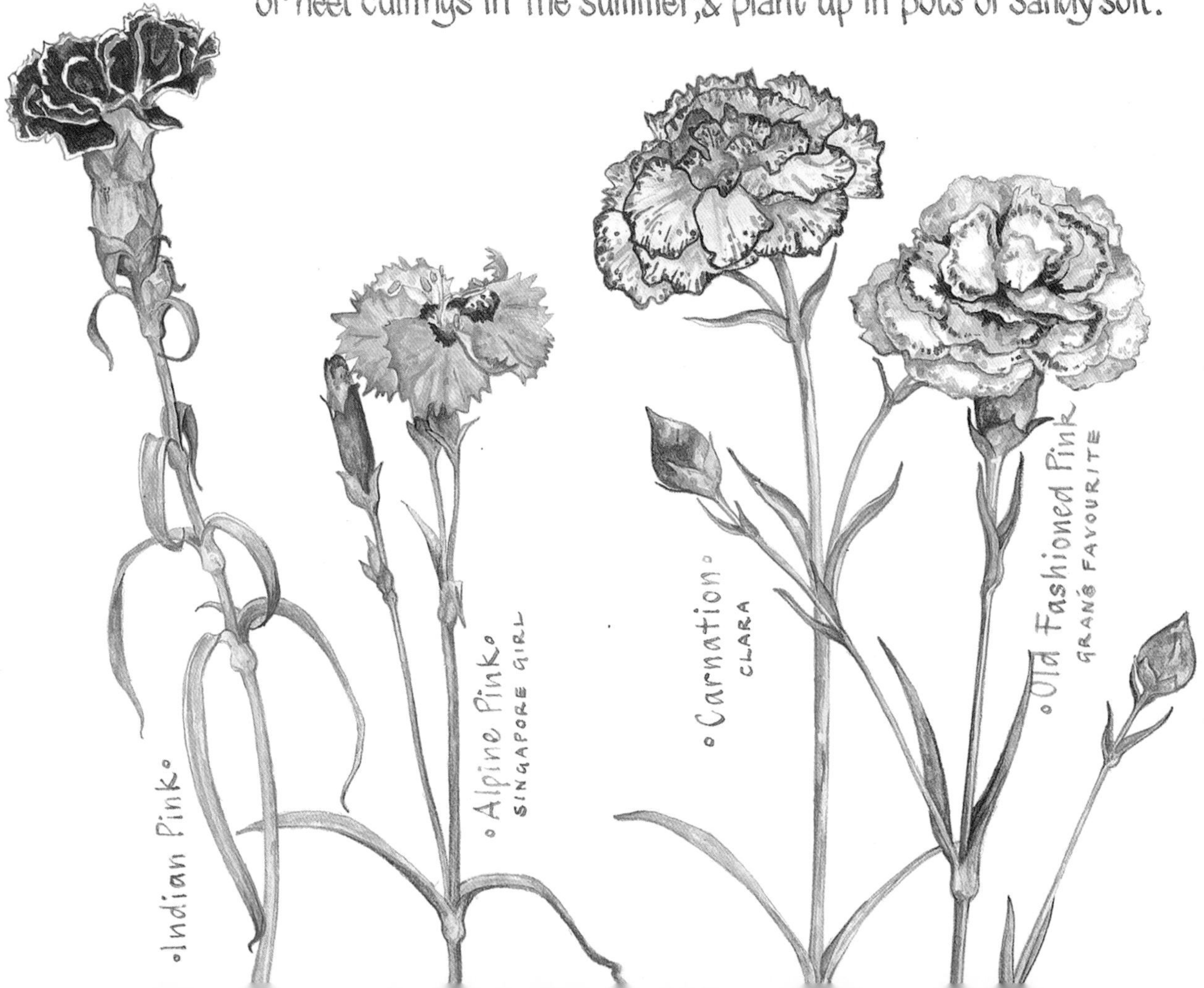

°Indian Pink°

°Alpine Pink°
SINGAPORE GIRL

°Carnation°
CLARA

°Old Fashioned Pink°
GRAN'S FAVOURITE

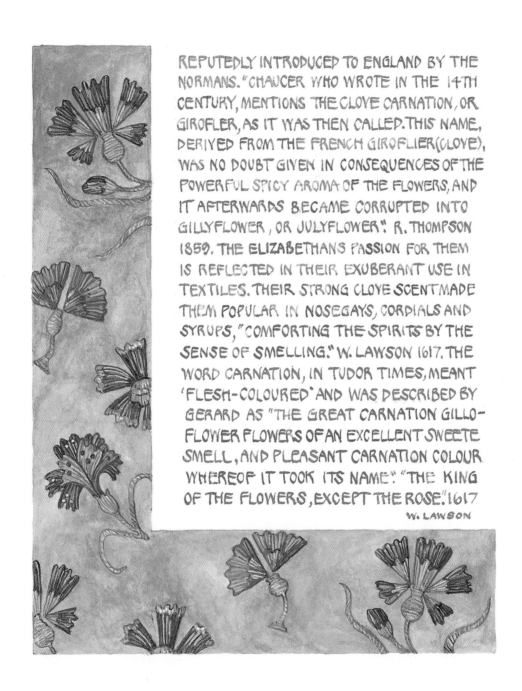

REPUTEDLY INTRODUCED TO ENGLAND BY THE NORMANS. "CHAUCER WHO WROTE IN THE 14TH CENTURY, MENTIONS THE CLOVE CARNATION, OR GIROFLER, AS IT WAS THEN CALLED. THIS NAME, DERIVED FROM THE FRENCH GIROFLIER (CLOVE), WAS NO DOUBT GIVEN IN CONSEQUENCES OF THE POWERFUL SPICY AROMA OF THE FLOWERS, AND IT AFTERWARDS BECAME CORRUPTED INTO GILLYFLOWER, OR JULYFLOWER". R. THOMPSON 1859. THE ELIZABETHANS PASSION FOR THEM IS REFLECTED IN THEIR EXUBERANT USE IN TEXTILES. THEIR STRONG CLOVE SCENT MADE THEM POPULAR IN NOSEGAYS, CORDIALS AND SYRUPS, "COMFORTING THE SPIRITS BY THE SENSE OF SMELLING." W. LAWSON 1617. THE WORD CARNATION, IN TUDOR TIMES, MEANT 'FLESH-COLOURED' AND WAS DESCRIBED BY GERARD AS "THE GREAT CARNATION GILLO-FLOWER FLOWERS OF AN EXCELLENT SWEETE SMELL, AND PLEASANT CARNATION COLOUR WHEREOF IT TOOK ITS NAME." "THE KING OF THE FLOWERS, EXCEPT THE ROSE." 1617

W. LAWSON

POPPY

"There is no flower can be more glorious than the poppy... but their ill smell & soon fading makes them less regarded"

J WORLIDGE 1677

Poppies self-seed happily but thin out the seedlings.

One opium poppy seed pod can contain up to 30,000 seeds. These can be used on cakes and bread. Greek athletes ate poppy seeds mixed with honey & wine. Opium, made from the sap, has been used for centuries.

Iceland poppies last well in water. Singe the end of each stem with a burning match, which prevents the sap draining away. Cut the Oriental poppy down to the ground after it has finished flowerin

PAPAVER SOMNIFERUM   PAPAVER ORIENTALE

PAPAVER RHOEAS   MECONOPSIS CAMBRICA

69

geranium

Not to be confused with pelargoniums, hardy geraniums are also called cranesbills, a reference to the long beak-shaped seedpods. A lovely group of perennials of over 140 species, cranesbills are tough & easy to grow. They grow happily in sun or shade. They produce lots of flowers in shades of blue, pink and white. To propagate, divide the clumps in spring or autumn. Geranium macrorrhizum & g. endressii make good ground cover planting. G. pratense (meadow cranesbill) is found in the wild but makes a lovely border plant. G. sanguineum, the bloody cranesbill, is so called not because of its bright pink flowers, but from its use in treating wounds. They look lovely with old fashioned roses.

71

NASTURTIUM

NIGELLA

COSMOS

TAGETES

NICOTIANA

Annuals only last a single season although some such as the poached egg plant (limnanthes) self-seed happily. Annuals are perfect for adding instant colour to the garden. Wait until all frosts are over before sowing the seed outside. Thin out the young seedlings to ensure sturdy plants. Most annuals like a sunny position, although some tolerate shade such as begonias and busy Lizzy. Support taller annuals with twiggy sticks. NASTURTIUMS flourish in poor soil. Sow seeds in situ. The edible leaves & flowers have a strong peppery flavour. NIGELLA or love-in-a-mist has been grown for centuries. The seed is best sown in the autumn in a sunny position. This pretty blue flower produces attractive seed pods. COSMOS is a native of Mexico. Sow seed in greenhouse in the late spring. Adding valuable height to the border, dead-head regularly for continuous flowers until autumn frosts kill it. TAGETES, the shorter French marigold & taller African marigold were once grown by the Aztecs and their aromatic smell makes them an effective companion plant to deter aphids. NICOTIANA or tobacco plant grows in sun or partial shade. The white variety has a strong spicy scent especially in the evenings.

Sweet peas — Lathyrus odoratus — were much loved by the Victorians. Natives of Italy, sweet peas, with their deliciously scented flowers, epitomise summer for many. Two wonderfully fragrant varieties are Painted Lady and Gwendoline. The modern Spencer sweet pea was developed from a larger frillier petalled variety found by the head gardener at Althorp. Sweet peas appreciate a deeply dug well manured fertile soil and a warm sunny position. Either sow seed in autumn, over-wintering in a coldframe, for early flowers, or sow in the green-house in early spring to plant out in late spring. Sweet peas are quite hardy so can be sown outside in the open in spring. Pinch out the growing tips for sturdy plants. Support these annual climbers on canes or trellis. Regular watering is most important. Pick the flowers diligently all summer long for lots of blooms and never let a seed pod develop or flowering will stop. There is also a pretty perennial sweet pea.

Sweet peas · Sweet peas · Sweet peas ·

Here are sweet peas, on tip-toe
for a flight:
With wings of gentle flush
o'er delicate white,
And taper fingers catching
at all things,
To bind them all about
with tiny rings.

J. Keats
1817

75

These gloriously scented plants were grown by the Romans who ate the bulbs & used them medicinally, particularly for treating corns.

The white trumpet lily, Lilium regale, was discovered in 1904 growing wild in an isolated valley in China. Martagon lilies can be naturalized in woodland conditions.

LILY · LILY · LILY · LILY · LILY · LILY · LILY · LILY

LILY · LILY · LILY · LILY · LILY · LILY · LILY · LILY

Most lilies are easy to grow. They like well drained soil & most thrive in sun. Lily bulbs should be plump & firm. Plant deeply in pots

or the border, except the Madonna lily which should be planted 1" deep in the autumn. This is one of the oldest cultivated flowers. "Give me lilies in armfuls" Virgil 70-19 B.C.

"OF A MOST PLEASANT GRATEFUL SCENT, SUCCEEDED BY SMALL ROUND RED BERRIES". W. CULPEPER

Climbers give height to the garden. They can be grown up fences, trellis, trees, walls, pergolas, obelisks, walls and wigwams. Some may need to be supported with wires. Honeysuckle is perfect for growing up arches and pergolas and is lovely combined with clematis & roses. Once known as woodbine, it has gloriously scented flowers. Roses such as the thornless scented climber Zephirine Drouhin are ideal for clothing arches. The more vigorous rambler roses will happily scramble through trees. Hydrangea petiolaris is a deciduous climber with pretty lace cap white flowers & is ideal for a north facing wall. Wisteria was brought from China in the early 1800s. Flowering in late spring, it needs to be pruned twice a year to control it. Virginia creeper leaves turn a rich glorious red before they fall in the autumn.

CLIMBERS

TO PRUNE CLEMATIS – IF IT BLOOMS AFTER JUNE, CUT BACK HARD TO 6" ABOVE THE GROUND; BEFORE JUNE, TRIM BACK SIDE SHOOTS AFTER FLOWERING.

"A hardy plant, common enough in gardens; it is a climber, and is suited to bowers & trellis work, or for other conspicuous places". W. Cobbett 1829. There are many different cultivars and species in a vast range of colours such as blue, lavender, purple, rose pink, carmine, burgundy and ruby red. The smaller flowering species are usually more vigorous than the larger flowering hybrids. The spring montanas will happily scramble through trees and over walls & roofs. Plant deeply so that the clematis can shoot again from the base if it suffers from clematis wilt. Plant in fertile soil & feed & water well. Clematis like their roots in the shade so surround with smaller shrubs or perennials or some stone slabs.

CLEMATIS

Herbes and Rootes for Sallets and Sauce

Alexanders, at all times. Artichoks. Blessed thistle, or Carduus benedictus. Cucumbers in April & May. Cresies, sowe with Lettice in the Spring. Endive, mustard seede, sowe in the Spring and Michelmas. Musk mullion in April and May. Mints. Purslane. Radish, & after remove them. Rampions. Rokat, in April. Sage. Sorell. Spinage for the sommer. Sea holie. Sperage, let growe two years, and then remove. Skirrets, set these plants in March. Suckerie, Tarragon, set in slippes in March. Violets of all coolors. These buie with the penie. Or looke not for anie. Capers, Lemmans. Olives. Orengis. Rise. Sampire. T. TUSSER 1580

CHIVES MAKE A PRETTY EDGING
PLANT. CUT RIGHT DOWN AFTER
FLOWERING AND THEY WILL SOON
REJUVENATE. PLANT NEXT TO ROSES
TO DETER APHIDS AND NEXT TO
APPLE TREES TO PREVENT SCAB.

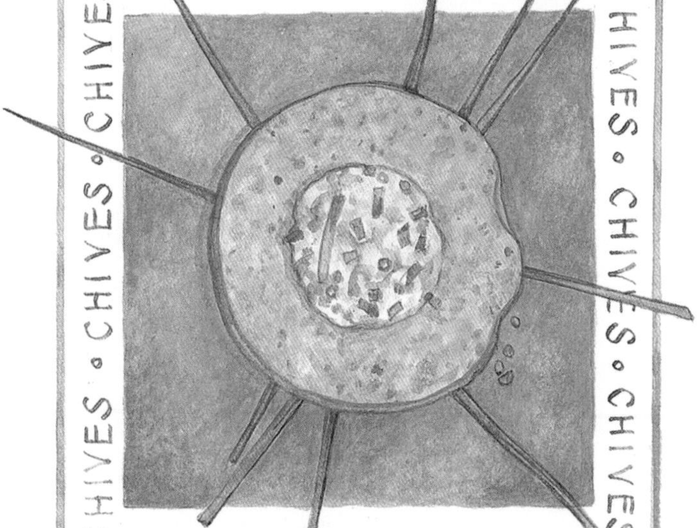

SNIP CHIVES OVER POTATO SALAD
OR EGG DISHES. TO MAKE CHIVE
BUTTER, MIX THE FINELY CHOPPED
CHIVES INTO SOFT BUTTER WITH
A LITTLE LEMON JUICE. MELT OVER
FISH OR SPREAD ONTO OAKCAKES.

• CHIVES • CHIVES • CHIVES • CHIVES • CHIVES •

• CHIVES • CHIVES • CHIVES • CHIVES • CHIVES •

Boil it in water, wet thy shirt with it and dry it again and wear it. LANGHAM 1579

There are many ways to enjoy lavender. Try lavender bath oil in a hot relaxing bath. Tea made from lavender is a good remedy for headaches. The bags perfume drawers and linen. Lavender honey is good on bread. Lavender adds a tasty tang to biscuits and sorbets. Lavender vinegar gives flavour to sauces and dressings. Pot pourri made from the dried flowers scents any room. The oil is used to relieve nervous tension and aches, and insect bites.

According to folklore, if lavender grows well, the daughters of the house won't marry

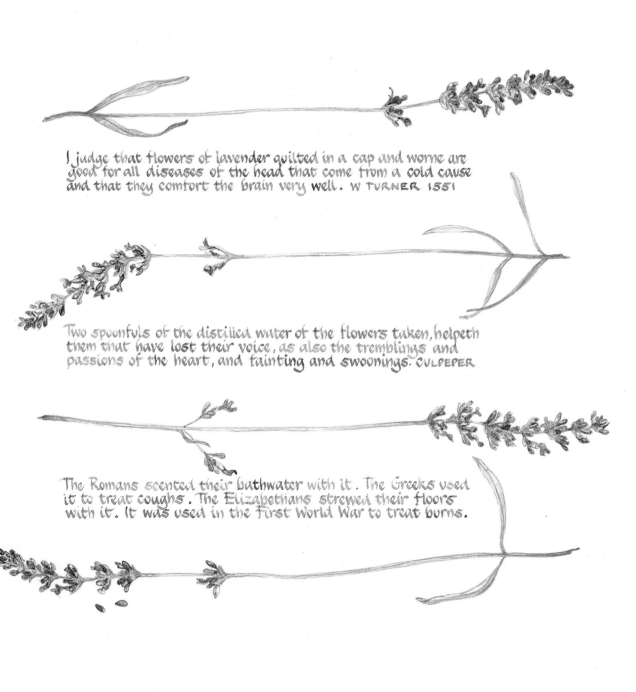

I judge that flowers of lavender quilted in a cap and worne are good for all diseases of the head that come from a cold cause and that they comfort the brain very well. W TURNER 1551

Two spoonfuls of the distilled water of the flowers taken, helpeth them that have lost their voice, as also the tremblings and passions of the heart, and fainting and swoonings. CULPEPER

The Romans scented their bathwater with it. The Greeks used it to treat coughs. The Elizabethans strewed their floors with it. It was used in the First World War to treat burns.

ROSEMARY LOVES A SUNNY WELL-DRAINED POSITION. IT BENEFITS FROM CLIPPING. USE THE CLIPPINGS IN YOUR COOKING. IT WAS ONCE USED IN BRIDAL BOUQUETS. IT WAS ALSO THROWN ONTO COFFINS BY MOURNERS. "IT MAKES THE HEART MERRY." N. CULPEPER 1652

ROSEMARY IS EFFECTIVE AS A MOTH REPELLENT AND A COUGH CURE. USE TO FLAVOUR VINEGAR & AS A HAIR RINSE FOR DARK HAIR. HANG A BUNCH UNDER THE HOT TAP TO INFUSE BATH WATER WITH ESSENTIAL OILS. "SMELL IT & IT SHALL KEEP THEE YOUNGLY" BANCKE 1525

dill

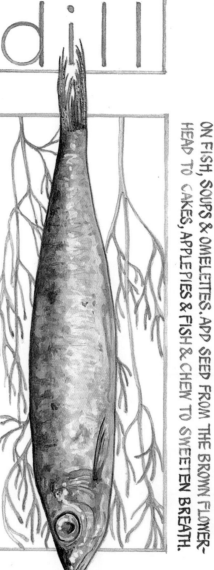

EARLY AMERICAN SETTLERS GAVE THEIR CHILDREN DILL SEEDS TO CHEW DURING LONG SERMONS, WHICH WERE CALLED 'MEETING SEEDS'. COLICKY BABES WERE COMFORTED WITH DILL WATER.

THIS ANNUAL ENJOYS FULL SUN. USE FINELY CHOPPED LEAVES ON FISH, SOUPS & OMELETTES. ADD SEED FROM THE BROWN FLOWER-HEAD TO CAKES, APPLE PIES & FISH & CHEW TO SWEETEN BREATH.

'IT STAYETH THE HICCOUGH.'
CULPEPER 1826

·bay·

LAURUS NOBILIS

·bay·

LAURUS NOBILIS

The Romans believed bay protected them from any thunderbolts, so Emperor Tiberius Caesar donned a wreath of it during thunder storms. It was also worn by the Ancients as a symbol of glory and victory. Planted near a house, it protected the occupants in days gone by from evil. A dying bay tree foretold disaster "Tis thought the king is dead; we will not stay. The bay trees in our country are all wither'd". Shakespeare Its strongly aromatic leaves make it popular in cooking and as an air-freshener. "The berries are very effectual against the poison of venemous creatures and the stings of wasps and bees". Culpeper 1826.

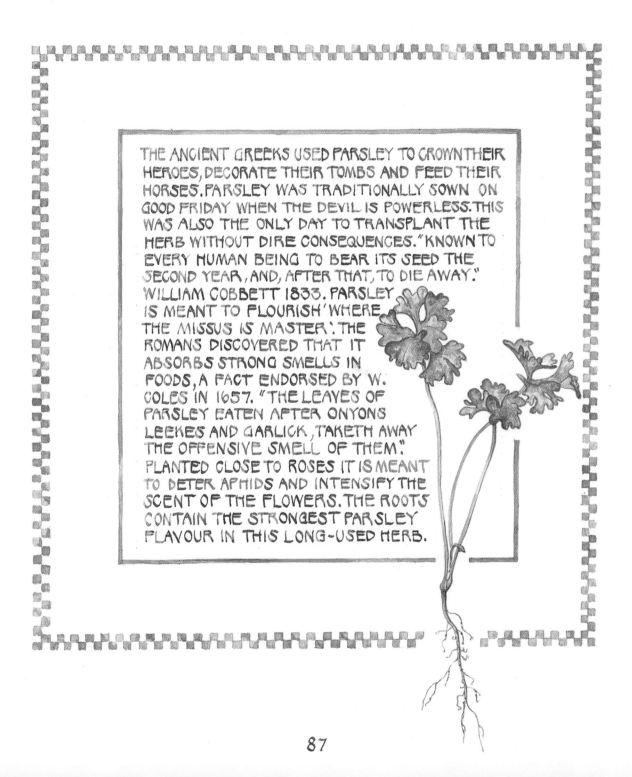

THE ANCIENT GREEKS USED PARSLEY TO CROWN THEIR
HEROES, DECORATE THEIR TOMBS AND FEED THEIR
HORSES. PARSLEY WAS TRADITIONALLY SOWN ON
GOOD FRIDAY WHEN THE DEVIL IS POWERLESS. THIS
WAS ALSO THE ONLY DAY TO TRANSPLANT THE
HERB WITHOUT DIRE CONSEQUENCES. "KNOWN TO
EVERY HUMAN BEING TO BEAR ITS SEED THE
SECOND YEAR, AND, AFTER THAT, TO DIE AWAY."
WILLIAM COBBETT 1833. PARSLEY
IS MEANT TO FLOURISH 'WHERE
THE MISSUS IS MASTER'. THE
ROMANS DISCOVERED THAT IT
ABSORBS STRONG SMELLS IN
FOODS, A FACT ENDORSED BY W.
COLES IN 1657. "THE LEAVES OF
PARSLEY EATEN AFTER ONYONS
LEEKES AND GARLICK, TAKETH AWAY
THE OFFENSIVE SMELL OF THEM".
PLANTED CLOSE TO ROSES IT IS MEANT
TO DETER APHIDS AND INTENSIFY THE
SCENT OF THE FLOWERS. THE ROOTS
CONTAIN THE STRONGEST PARSLEY
FLAVOUR IN THIS LONG-USED HERB.

MINT

There are more than 600 varieties – ginger, applemint, spearmint, black peppermint, eau de cologne & lemon among them. To control its vigorous growth, plant in a bottomless pot. Grows happily in sun or partial shade. Dig out if it has rust. Grow near roses to deter aphids, & near cabbages to deter cabbage white butterflies. Mint was rubbed onto skin by the ancient Greeks as a deodorant. The leaves make a refreshing tea which calms the stomach. Chewing the leaves freshens the breath. "The French snip a little in their salads; we boil a bunch amongst green peas ... we use it as a sauce for roasted lamb; and a very pleasant sauce it is." WILLIAM COBBETT 1833

EAU DE COLOGNE
MINT

Basil is revered by the Hindus. Its aromatic clove-like scent increases in flavour when cooked. It is particularly

good with tomatoes. A pot on the kitchen windowsill will deter flies. The powdered leaves were once used as snuff.

89

·SAGE·   ·BORAGE·

·THYME·   ·MARJORAM·

90

Sage tea was drunk by the medieval English as a cure-all. "Why should a man die when sage grows in his garden". Sage tea is still used as an effective gargle for sore throats. This evergreen looks lovely in a flower border and likes a sunny well-drained position.

·SAGE·

Loved by bees, this annual self-seeds very happily. Pull out unwanted plants. "If once you have it growing upon any spot, you need not trouble to sow it". W. Cobbett 1829. Add the chopped cucumber-tasting leaves and flowers to summer drinks & salads.

·BORAGE·

Beer and thyme soup was once consumed as a cure for shyness. "It is so harmless you need not fear the use of it". Culpeper 1826 Thyme comes in very many varieties & likes a sunny well drained soil. Cut back hard after flowering. "It smelleth comfortably". 1617
W. LAWSON

·THYME·

The Greek symbol for peace and happiness, this aromatic herb is adored by bees & butterflies. It dries & freezes well. Add to pizza, egg and cheese dishes. "The leaves boiled in water, & the decoction drunke, easeth such as are given to overmuch sighing".
GERARD 1597

·MARJORAM·

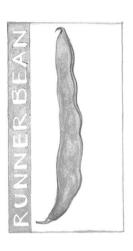

RUNNER BEAN

A NATIVE OF MEXICO, RUNNER BEANS WERE OFTEN GROWN FOR THEIR DECORATIVE FLOWERS WHEN THEY WERE FIRST INTRODUCED TO EUROPE. "IT FLOWRETH ALL SUMMER ALMOST". SIR T. HANMER .1659. A TENDER ANNUAL, SOW AFTER THE LAST FROSTS IN A PREPARED TRENCH FILLED WITH COMPOST, MANURE OR SOAKED NEWS-PAPER TO HELP RETAIN MOISTURE. PICK WHEN YOUNG AND TENDER. KEEP PICKING FOR A CONTINUOUS CROP. THEY DO NOT THRIVE NEXT TO BRASSICAS & ONIONS.

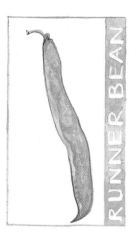

RUNNER BEAN

PARSNIP

"IN THE NORTH OF SCOTLAND, PARSNIPS ARE OFTEN BEAT UP WITH POTATOES & A LITTLE BUTTER; OF THIS EXCELLENT MESS THE CHILDREN OF THE PEASANTRY ARE VERY FOND, & THEY DO NOT FAIL TO THRIVE UPON IT". P. NEILL 1821. SOW SEED GENEROUSLY IN LATE SPRING. GERMINATION CAN BE ERRATIC, & THE CROP MATURES SLOWLY. PLANT RADISH & LETTUCE BETWEEN ROWS. HARVEST IN AUTUMN AFTER THE FIRST FROSTS FOR A BETTER FLAVOUR — WHICH TURNS SOME OF THEIR STARCH INTO SUGAR.

PARSNIP

CABBAGE

ONCE CALLED ' THE POOR MAN'S DOCTOR', CABBAGE WAS ONCE USED TO CURE MANY AILMENTS SUCH AS BRONCHITIS AND WORMS. LEAVES, COOKED IN MILK, WERE COOLED & APPLIED TO BLISTERS. PLANT NEXT TO POTATOES AND ONIONS. CABBAGES LIKE A RICH FERTILE SOIL AND A SUNNY SPOT. VARIOUS TYPES OF CABBAGES CAN BE HARVESTED ALL THE YEAR ROUND, AND SOME ARE INDEED BEAUTIFUL ENOUGH TO BE GROWN IN THE FLOWER BORDER.

CABBAGE

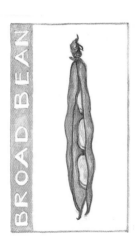

BROAD BEAN

EATEN SINCE PREHISTORIC TIMES, BROAD BEANS WERE THE STAPLE DIET OF THE POOR. PLANT THE SEED OUTSIDE IN LATE AUTUMN OR EARLY SPRING. PINCH OUT TIPS WHEN PLANTS ARE IN FLOWER TO DETER BLACKFLY INFESTATION. SUPPORT TALLER VARIETIES WITH STICKS & STRING. PICK THE PODS WHEN SMALL FOR A TENDER TASTY BEAN. BROAD BEANS GROW WELL NEXT TO POTATOES, THE BEAN FIXES NITROGEN IN THE SOIL WHICH POTATOES LIKE. THE FLOWERS' STRONG SCENT WAS THOUGHT TO INDUCE NIGHTMARES & MADNESS.

BROAD BEAN

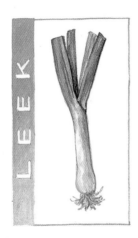

LEEK

ROMAN SINGERS ATE LEEKS TO IMPROVE THEIR VOICES. THE EMPEROR NERO WAS APPARENTLY A GREAT FAN OF LEEK SOUP. "THE WELCH, WHO EAT THEM MUCH, ARE OBSERV'D TO BE VERY FRUITFUL." J. EVELYN 1699. VERY HARDY, LEEKS CAN BE LEFT IN THE GROUND DURING THE WINTER, LIFTING WHEN REQUIRED. LEEKS NEED A FERTILE WELL-DRAINED SOIL AND ARE EASY TO GROW NEEDING LITTLE ATTENTION. WONDERFUL SEEDHEADS ARE PRODUCED. LEEKS ARE DELICIOUS IN SOUPS & TARTS.

LEEK

LETTUCE

"LETTUCE IS LIKE CONVERSATION: IT MUST BE FRESH & CRISP, SO SPARKLING THAT YOU SCARCELY NOTICE THE BITTER IN IT." C DUDLEY WARNER 1871. ITS SOPORIFIC PROPERTIES GAVE IT THE NAME SLEEPWORT. IT WAS EATEN AFTER MEALS TO PREVENT DRUNKENESS, AND STOMACH ACHES WERE TREATED WITH BOILED LETTUCE. SOW LETTUCE LITTLE AND OFTEN FOR A CONTINUOUS SUPPLY THROUGHOUT THE SUMMER. IT GROWS HAPPILY IN LIGHT SHADE IN FERTILE SOIL. WATER IT WELL.

LETTUCE

Green Peas, to Stew

Put into a pan 2lb peas, a lettuce, and an onion sliced, butter, pepper, salt, but no more water than remains about the lettuce after washing. Cook very gently until done.

The Best of Everything 1875

Peas

Peas were served as a refreshment during the interval of Roman and Greek plays. Before Tudor times peas were first dried and then boiled to make pease pudding. Peas were known as the 'Prince of the Vegetable Garden' during Victorian times. They were one of the first vegetables to be tinned, but were a hazard to health from the copper salts added to make the peas green. To find a pod containing nine peas was thought extremely lucky. They were also used as one of the many cures for warts. Peas thrive in the vegetable patch when planted next to leeks and carrots, but not near onions. 'Peas, when green, are a pleasant, grateful, nourishing food, but somewhat flatulent and windy. Culpeper 1826. 'Good gardiner mine, Make garden fine. Set garden pease, and beans if ye please. Tusser 1580

Radishes have been grown for thousands of years. There are summer & winter varieties; the former grow best in partial shade where they do not bolt so quickly. Radishes take 3-4 weeks to mature so sow regularly for continuous pickings, and eat when

young & tender. Thin the seedlings to 1" apart. Ideally grown as a catch crop between rows of slower growing vegetables. "In all sowings of radishes, the greatest care must be taken to keep away the birds... The sparrows will see you when you are sowing, will know very well what you are at." W COBBETT 1829

BETA VULGARIS · BETA VULGARIS

Wash the beetroot seeds well or soak overnight before sowing to encourage germination, but do not sow too early in the season or the plants will bolt. Harvest the beets when small. Beetroot likes a fertile soil but not one that has been freshly manured. Twist the leaves off the beetroot away from the crown to prevent any bleeding. "In the kitchen they must be only washed & not scraped, as, if the outer skin should be removed, all the colouring matter will escape when the root is boiled, and the root, instead of its being of its usual bright red, will be of a dingy whitish pink". Jane Loudon 1845. There are different varieties of beetroot – round, long, yellow, white, two tone red with white rings & different shades of purplish red. The leaves are also edible.

BEETROOT · BEETROOT · BEETROOT

TOMATO

THE NAME COMES FROM THE AZTEC WORD 'TOMATL'. IN ENGLAND IT WAS GROWN INITIALLY AS A DECORATIVE PLANT FROM THE 1500's, AND LATER IT WAS ONLY THOUGHT SAFE TO EAT WHEN COOKED. IT WAS CALLED THE LOVE-APPLE AS IT WAS CONSIDERED AN APHRODISIAC. TOMATOES COME IN MANY SHAPES INCLUDING OVAL AND RIBBED, AND MANY COLOURS ~ ORANGE, YELLOW & BLACK AMONGST OTHERS AND EVEN STRIPED. SIZE VARIES FROM TINY CHERRY TOMATOES TO THE HUGE OXHEART TYPES. PLANT OUT SEEDS RAISED IN THE GREENHOUSE WHEN ALL RISK OF FROST HAS PASSED. PLANT WITH BASIL OR TAGETES TO DETER APHIDS BUT AVOID PLANTING NEAR BRASSICAS OR POTATOES.

"HAVE YOU ANY TOMATAS?   FANNY
AND I REGALE ON THEM EVERY DAY."

JANE AUSTEN 1813

·STRAWBERRY·

FRAGARIA ANANASSA

Plant in a sunny, well drained spot, in well-manured soil 18" apart. Renew plants every three years. Tuck clean straw under plants when the fruit starts to develop. Cover with netting to deter birds and any hungry children! After fruiting cut the leaves right back to within a few inches of the crown. Edge paths and vegetable beds with alpine strawberries.

Doubtless God could have made a better berry, but doubtless God never did.
W. Butler 1661

Wife, into thy garden, and set me a plot, with strawberry rootes, of the best to be got. Tusser 1580

They will cool my Housewife well, if they be put in wine and cream with Sugar.
W Lawson 1617

No man ever having found that he had too much of this excellent fruit.
W Cobbett 1833

They will cool my Housewife well, if they be put in wine and cream with Sugar.

Dreaming of strawberries is good luck. For a man it fortells a quiet wife and a large family.

The water of the berries is good to fasten loose teeth, and to heal spungy foul gums
N Culpeper 1826

Among strawberries sow here and there some borage seed and you shall find the strawberries under those leaves farre more larger than their fellowes
W Coles 1656

A cut strawberry will whiten the skin, particularly when sunburnt. The juice will also clean dis-coloured teeth.

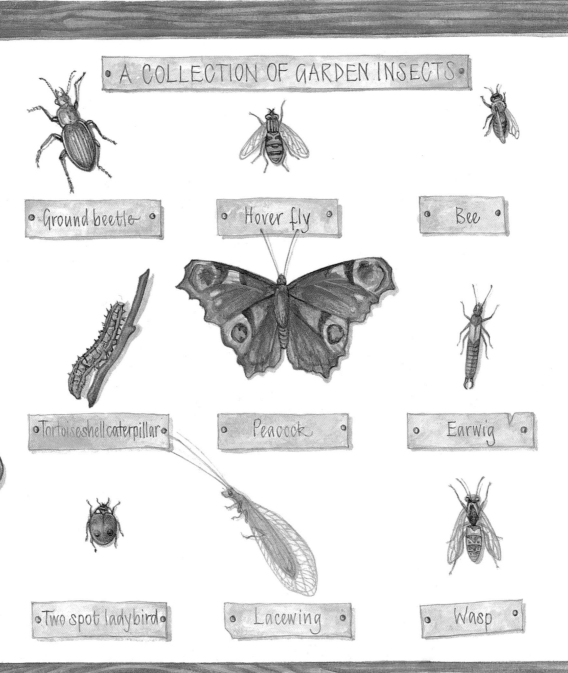

A COLLECTION OF GARDEN INSECTS

Ground beetle

Hover fly

Bee

Tortoiseshell caterpillar

Peacock

Earwig

Two spot ladybird

Lacewing

Wasp

• Cabbage White •

"AS THE WARM WEATHER PROGRESSES, THE GARDENER SHOULD BE ON THE ALERT IN ORDER TO CONQUER THE VARIOUS KINDS OF INSECTS". THE KITCHEN GARDENER'S INSTRUCTOR, 1860.

○ HOVERFLY ○ ITS HOVERING FLIGHT DISTINGUISHES IT FROM BEES AND WASPS. ITS LARVAE FEASTS ON APHIDS. ATTRACT INTO THE GARDEN WITH POACHED EGG PLANTS, HERBS, LAVENDER, NEPETA, COSMOS AND HONEYSUCKLE.

○ CABBAGE WHITE BUTTERFLY ○ PLANT FRENCH MARIGOLDS WITH CABBAGES TO DETER. NASTURTIUMS ARE ALSO EATEN BY THEIR CATERPILLARS SO PLANT NEARBY AS A DISTRACTION. ○ PEACOCK BUTTERFLY ○ THIS AND SEVERAL OTHER BUTTERFLIES LAY THEIR EGGS ON NETTLES SO LEAVE A PATCH IN THE GARDEN. BUTTERFLIES ALSO ENJOY FEEDING ON WINDFALL APPLES. BUTTERFLIES LIKE HONESTY, SEDUM, HERBS, HONEYSUCKLE, BERGAMOT, CANDYTUFT, SCABIOUS & BUDDLEIA. ○ TORTOISESHELL CATERPILLAR ○ IT IS WISE TO REMEMBER BEFORE DESTROYING THEM THAT CATERPILLARS TURN INTO BUTTERFLIES AND MOTHS. ○ GROUND BEETLE ○ THE GARDENER'S FRIENDS, GROUND BEETLES FEED ON SLUGS AND PLANT-CONSUMING INSECTS AT NIGHT. LEAVE GROUND COVER SUCH AS LOGS AND STONES FOR THEM TO HIDE UNDER. ○ EARWIG ○ THE EARWIG NIBBLES FLOWERS & BUDS SO TRAP IN AN UPSIDE DOWN FLOWER POT ON A CANE STUFFED WITH LEAVES OR DRIED GRASS. ○ LACEWING ○ A BENEFICIAL INSECT, THE LARVAE DEVOUR APHIDS SO ENCOURAGE THE ADULT WITH POACHED EGG PLANTS, MARIGOLDS & SUNFLOWERS. ADULTS ALSO ENJOY A GOOD MEAL OF APHIDS. ○ LADYBIRD ○ BOTH ADULTS & LARVAE EAT HUGE QUANTITIES OF APHIDS. ATTRACT THESE EXCELLENT INSECTS WITH GOOD MIXED PLANTING. THEY HIBERNATE OVER THE WINTER. ○ WASP ○ A BENEFICIAL INSECT EARLY IN THE SEASON WHEN THEY HUNT OTHER INSECTS. TRAP IN LATE SUMMER, WHEN THEY DAMAGE FRUIT, IN JAM JARS FILLED WITH CIDER, BEER OR ANYTHING SWEET. ○ BEE ○ ESSENTIAL FOR POLLINATION, ONLY THE FEMALE HONEY BEE OR WORKER HAS A STING & WORKS SO HARD SHE SELDOM LIVES FOR LONGER THAN A MONTH. RUB A BEE STING WITH AN ONION OR A MARIGOLD AFTER REMOVING THE STING.

AUTUMN

SEASON OF MISTS AND MELLOW FRUITFULNESS

KEATS

SEASONAL TASKS

- PLANT SPRING FLOWERING BULBS
- TAKE HARDWOOD CUTTINGS OF SHRUBS
- MOVE PLANTS WHERE NECESSARY
- LIFT AND DIVIDE PERENNIALS
- CLEAR UP DEAD LEAVES AND STORE FOR LEAF MOULD
- COLLECT SEEDS AND STORE IN A DRY CONTAINER
- PLANT NEW TREES AND SHRUBS
- CHECK TREE TIES AND STAKES
- PRUNE CLIMBING AND RAMBLING ROSES
- SOW SWEET PEAS IN A COLD FRAME
- LEAVE PEA AND BEAN ROOTS IN THE SOIL
- LIFT AND STORE ONIONS AND POTATOES
- PICK AND STORE APPLES, PEARS AND QUINCES

AUTUMN

· IVY ·

· LEYCESTERIA ·

· SOLOMON'S SEAL ·

· MISTLETOE ·

· COTONEASTER ·

· BERBERIS THUNBERGII ·

· ROSE ·

· FUCHSIA ·

· SNOWBERRY ·

· HONEYSUCKLE ·

· PYRACANTHA ·

· VIBURNUM ·

· HYPERICUM ·

· SORBUS ·

· DEADLY NIGHTSHADE ·

· SKIMMIA ·

· SPINDLE TREE ·

· ARBUTUS ·

· BERBERIS DARWINII ·

· LILY OF THE VALLEY ·

BERRIES

BERRIES ARE ONE OF THE GREAT DELIGHTS OF THE AUTUMN GARDEN, COMBINING SPECTAC- ULARLY WITH THE GLOWING HUES OF BURNISHED LEAVES. LATER THEY BRIGHTEN UP THE DULL DAYS OF WINTER, PROVIDING INTEREST IN THE GARDEN AND MUCH NEEDED FOOD FOR HUNGRY BIRDS. "WHEN TREES AND HEDGES ARE VERY FULL OF BERRIES, IT INDICATES A HARD WINTER". W. HONE 1826 ." BUT THE HEDGES... ARE NOW SPARKLING WITH THEIR ABUNDANT BERRIES – THE WILD ROSE WITH THE HIP, THE HAWTHORN WITH THE HAW, THE BLACKTHORN WITH THE SLOE, THE BRAMBLE WITH THE BLACKBERRY; & THE BRIONY, PRIVET, HONEY–SUCKLE, ELDER, HOLLY, AND WOODY NIGHT–SHADE, WITH THEIR OTHER WINTER FEASTS FOR THE BIRDS". L. HUNT 1821

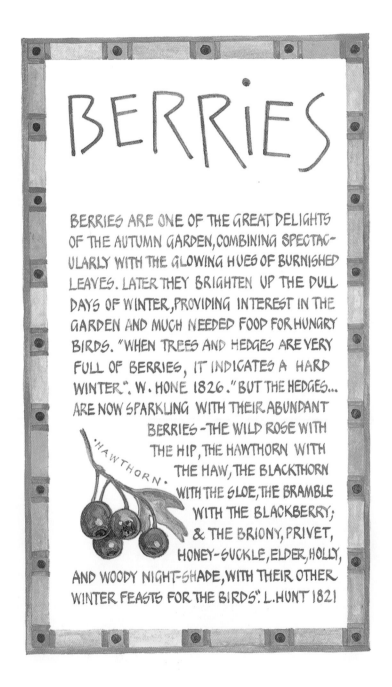

. HAWTHORN .

RoseHiPS

THE FRUIT OF THE ROSE, THE HIP, IS EXTREMELY HIGH IN VITAMIN C. DURING WORLD WAR II, WHEN CITRUS FRUITS WERE SCARCE, BRITISH CHILDREN WERE GIVEN ROSE HIP SYRUP. IN THE PAST, HIPS WERE USED IN SOUPS, PUDDINGS, JAMS & WINE & WERE USED TO TREAT SORE THROATS & COUGHS. ROSES WITH VERY ATTRACTIVE HIPS ARE THE RUGOSAS, RAMBLERS SUCH AS KIFTSGATE & RAMBLING RECTOR, ROSA GLAUCA & ROSA MOYESII.

RoseHiPS

TAKE HIPS, CUT THEM AND TAKE
OUT THE SEEDS VERY CLEAN, THEN
WASH THEM AND SEASON THEM

ROSE · HIP · TART

WITH SUGAR, CINNAMON AND
GINGER, CLOSE THE TART, BAKE
IT SCRAPE ON SUGAR AND ~
SERVE IT. ROBERT MAY 1671.

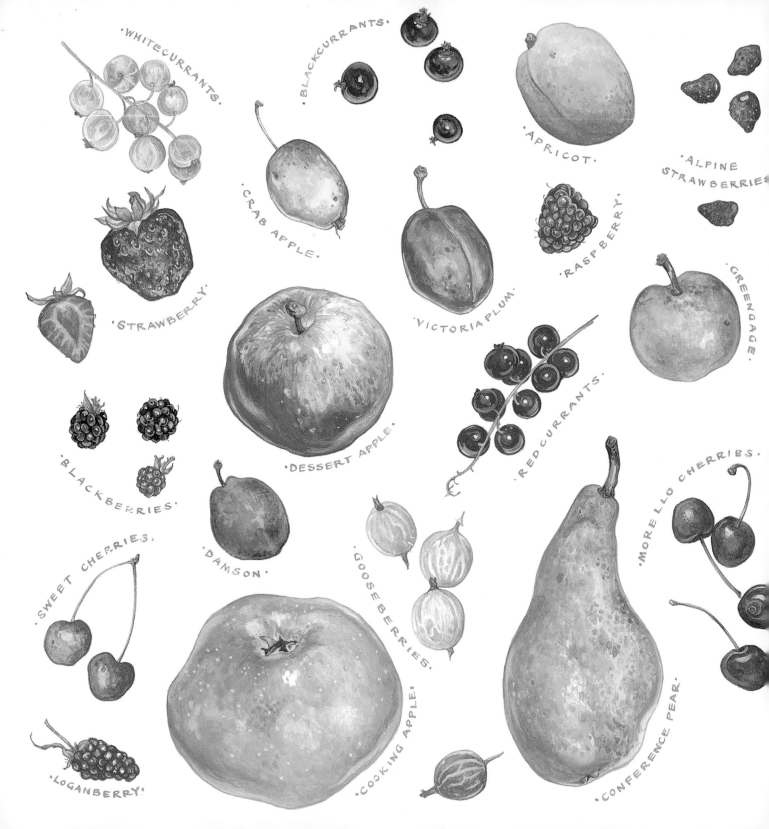

·WHITECURRANTS·

·BLACKCURRANTS·

·APRICOT·

·ALPINE STRAWBERRIES·

·CRAB APPLE·

·VICTORIA PLUM·

·RASPBERRY·

·GREENGAGE·

·STRAWBERRY·

·DESSERT APPLE·

·REDCURRANTS·

·MORELLO CHERRIES·

·BLACKBERRIES·

·SWEET CHERRIES·

·DAMSON·

·GOOSEBERRIES·

·CONFERENCE PEAR·

·LOGANBERRY·

·COOKING APPLE·

SCHOLA SALERNI ADVISES TO DRINK
MUCH WINE AFTER PEARS, OR ELSE
(SAY THEY) THEY ARE AS BAD AS
POISON, AND THEY CURSE THE TREE
FOR IT TOO. NICHOLAS CULPEPER

IN MEDIEVAL AND ELIZABETHAN TIMES, PEARS,
LIKE MOST FRUITS, WERE WELL COOKED IN SUGAR,
SPICES, AND OFTEN RED WINE, TO AID DIGESTION.
"FRUITES GENERALLY ARE NOYFULLE TO MAN AND
DO INGENDER ILL HUMOURS" SIR THOMAS ELYOT 1541

Red Williams.

I NEVER PERCEIVED MY CATTLE EXTREMELY ANXIOUS
ABOUT OTHER FRUIT, BUT TO GET AT THE PERRY PEARS
THE STEERS AND OXEN USED TO RAISE THEMSELVES
UPON THEIR HIND-LEGS, WHICH I VERY RARELY SAW THEM
DO IN THE CASE OF ANY OTHER TREE. W. COBBETT 1829

THE PEAR WAS GROWN AND ENJOYED
BY THE ROMANS AND GREEKS. SINCE
THEN, OVER 5,000 VARIETIES HAVE
BEEN DEVELOPED IN EUROPE AND
AMERICA. "PLANT PEARS FOR YOUR HEIRS."

An apple eaten at midnight on Halloween is meant to prevent the consumer from catching a cold for a year. Apple juice was applied to noses reddened by drink to reduce the fiery glow. Country folk would leave a few apples on trees for the fairies to bring good luck to the household. A long strip of peel thrown over the left shoulder will spell out the initials of a future spouse. Wassailing the apple tree was carried out on Twelfth Night to ensure a good crop. Cider was poured over the roots of a chosen tree, and all assembled drank to it. Toast was hung in the branches for the robin, a bringer of fortune. Shots were fired into the tree to drive away evil spirits. Beating the tree was also thought to help its future performance. 'The more ripe ones eaten raw move the belly a little; and unripe ones have the contrary effect'. N. Culpeper 1826 'If Fruit stand too long it will be mealy, which is worse than shrively, for now most Gentlemen chuse the shriveled Apple'. Hillman 1710

IN ELIZABETHAN TIMES COLOURED LIQUID WAS POURED INTO HOLES BORED INTO THE APPLE TREES TRUNKS TO HELP THE TREES PRODUCE THE REQUIRED YELLOW, RED OR GREEN FRUIT. HAMMERING IRON NAILS INTO

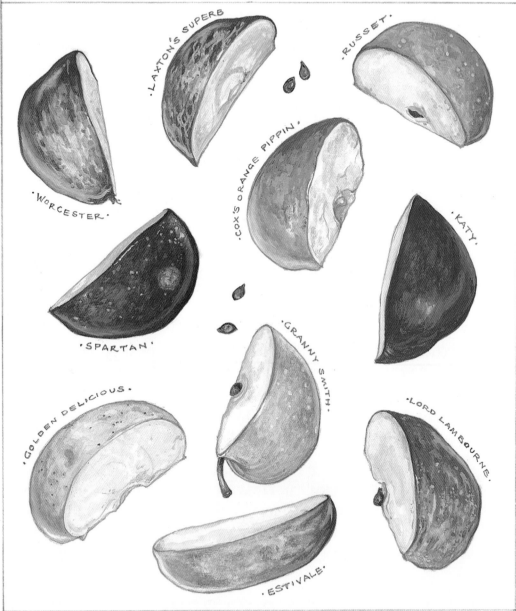

·LAXTON'S SUPERB

·RUSSET·

·WORCESTER·

·COX'S ORANGE PIPPIN·

·KATY·

·SPARTAN·

·GRANNY SMITH·

·GOLDEN DELICIOUS·

·LORD LAMBOURNE·

·ESTIVALE·

THE TRUNKS WAS DONE TO ENCOURAGE THE TREES TO CROP WELL, WITH THE ADDITIONAL BENEFIT OF DRIVING WITCHES AWAY. RED ROSES GROWN NEAR AN APPLE TREE PRODUCES RED FRUIT.

Alpine strawberries, used in Victorian fruit salads, were also used to edge flower beds. The cultivated strawberry first came to Britain in the 1500's. "I have already fifteen varieties of strawberries; and I have no idea if I had hit on the right one... Oh, for the good old days when a strawberry was a strawberry, and there was no perplexity about it." C. DUDLEY WARNER 1876

The medlar was very popular in past times. It can only be eaten when over-ripe or bletted. Traditionally it was roasted with butter and cloves. It was supposed to improve the memory. "It is hardly worth notice, being, at best, only one degree better than a rotten apple." W. COBBETT 1829. The hardy self-fertile tree, introduced to Britain in 995, blossoms in midsummer.

The gooseberry is possibly named after the prickly bush's similarity to the spiky gorse, hence gorse berry. It may also have derived from the goose-berry sauce served with roast goose. Lindley's Guide to the Orchard and Kitchen Garden of 1831 lists more than 700 varieties. Grown in gardens since 1200's, competitive growing later caused Gooseberry Clubs to flourish.

Collecting blackberries in the autumn is one of the few pleasures we share with Neolithic man! It is supposedly unlucky to eat blackberries after 11 October whereafter the fruit is cursed by the Devil, who, when he was thrown out of Heaven, fell into the thorny bush. Walking backwards through an arch of brambles will cure boils, it is said.

Figs were brought to England by the Romans. Despite the pollution of 17th century London, fig trees grew and fruited well. Twenty four kinds were listed a century ago, few except Brown Turkey remain today. "An ointment made from the juice and hog's grease is as excellent a remedy for the biting of mad-dogs, or other venemous beasts." CULPEPER 1826

·STRAWBERRY·MEDLAR·GOOSEBERRY·BLACKBERRY·FIG·

Quinces were called apples of Cydonia (or Crete) by the Greeks, which today is still reflected in its botanical name. They were eaten, covered in honey, at Roman weddings. "There is no fruit growing in this Land that is of so many excellent uses as this, serving as well to make many dishes of meate for the table, as for banquets, and much more for the Physicall vertues. PARKINSON

Mulberry trees can live many 100's of years. The white mulberry was brought to England from China to provide leaves for silk worms to feed on. To gather mulberries inevitably stains the hands of the gatherer red, a fact recorded by Shakespeare. It is the last tree in the orchard to blossom, and consequently was revered by the ancients as the wisest tree.

One hundred and fifty seven cherry trees were planted in Queen Henrietta Maria's garden, enjoyed as much for their beauty as for their fruit. In Tudor times a bowl of cherries was a very acceptable present. "Your Cherries, and other Berries, when they be ripe, will draw all the Black-birds, Thrushes and Mag-pies to your Orchard. W LAWSON 1618.

Blackcurrants were once called quinsy berries, and have been grown since about 15th century in cottage gardens. The leaves are very strongly scented and particularly attractive to goats! " Both branches leaves and fruit have a kind of stinking sent with them, yet are not unwholesome, but are eaten of many, without offending either taste or smell. J PARKINSON 1629

The plum has been cultivated for over 2000 years in Europe. Greengages are thought to be the best of the plums, named after Sir William Gage who brought the fruit over from France in 1724. "For a mouth troubled with eruption within: take leaves of a plum tree, boil in wine and swill the mouth therewith." Leechbook of Bald c. 900.

·QUINCE·MULBERRY· CHERRY·BLACKCURRANT·PLUM·

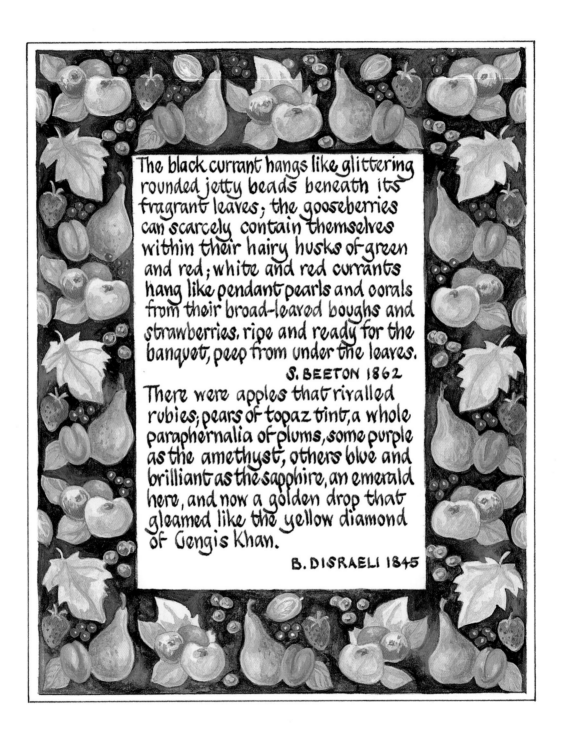

The black currant hangs like glittering rounded jetty beads beneath its fragrant leaves; the gooseberries can scarcely contain themselves within their hairy husks of green and red; white and red currants hang like pendant pearls and corals from their broad-leaved boughs and strawberries, ripe and ready for the banquet, peep from under the leaves.

S. BEETON 1862

There were apples that rivalled rubies; pears of topaz tint, a whole paraphernalia of plums, some purple as the amethyst, others blue and brilliant as the sapphire, an emerald here, and now a golden drop that gleamed like the yellow diamond of Gengis Khan.

B. DISRAELI 1845

CRAB APPLE · CRABAPPLE

CRABAPPLE JELLY

COOK 5 LBS CRAB APPLES WITH
3 PINTS OF WATER FOR ABOUT
AN HOUR UNTIL IT IS REDUCED
TO A PULP. STRAIN THIS MASH
THROUGH A JELLY BAG. BOIL
EACH PINT OF JUICE WITH 1 LB
SUGAR UNTIL A SET
IS REACHED. POUR
INTO HOT CLEAN
JARS. COVER.

CRABAPPLE · CRABAPPLE

•POTATO•

THE POTATO WAS SOLD FOR HUGE PRICES IN 16TH
CENTURY SPAIN AS A CURE FOR IMPOTENCE. IN 1728
THE CULTIVATION OF THE POTATO WAS PROHIBITED IN
SCOTLAND OWING TO ITS OMISSION FROM THE BIBLE,
ALTHOUGH BY 1773 SAMUEL JOHNSON REPORTED ON
A VISIT TO THE SCOTTISH HIGHLANDS, "POTATOES
AT LEAST ARE NEVER WANTING, WHICH, THOUGH THEY
HAVE NOT KNOWN THEM LONG, ARE NOW ONE OF THE
PRINCIPAL PARTS OF THEIR FOOD."
ACCORDING TO FOLKLORE, A POTATO CARRIED IN THE
POCKET CURED TOOTHACHE AS WELL AS RHEUMATISM.
THIS WORKED BETTER IF IT WAS STOLEN. POTATOES
DUG UP AFTER SUNSET WERE SUPPOSED NOT TO ROT
"PLANT YOUR POTATOES WHEN THE MOON IS ON THE
WANE, THEY WANT TO GROW DOWN, THAT IS PLAIN",
A VICTORIAN BIRD SCARER CONSISTED OF WHITE FEATHERS
STUCK INTO A POTATO & HUNG OVER THE VEGETABLE
PATCH ON A RED THREAD.

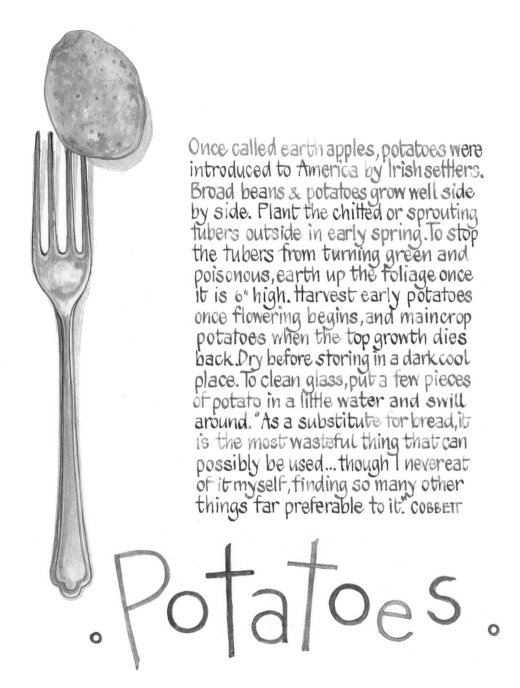

Once called earth apples, potatoes were introduced to America by Irish settlers. Broad beans & potatoes grow well side by side. Plant the chitted or sprouting tubers outside in early spring. To stop the tubers from turning green and poisonous, earth up the foliage once it is 6" high. Harvest early potatoes once flowering begins, and maincrop potatoes when the top growth dies back. Dry before storing in a dark cool place. To clean glass, put a few pieces of potato in a little water and swill around. "As a substitute for bread, it is the most wasteful thing that can possibly be used...though I never eat of it myself, finding so many other things far preferable to it." COBBETT

.Potatoes.

PUMPKIN SEED IMPROVES WITH AGE, OLD SEED PRODUCES MORE FEMALE FLOWERS. THEY GROW ENORMOUSLY WELL IN COMPOST.

DO NOT WASTE THE NUMEROUS SEEDS IN A PUMPKIN. ROAST THEM IN A MODERATE OVEN IN A LITTLE OIL & SALT - DELICIOUS.

SWEET DUMPLING   TURK'S CAP   KABOCHA SQUASH

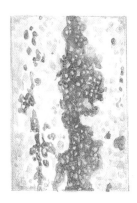  

PUMPKINS "ARE OF VARIOUS SORTS,
THE FRUIT OF SOME OF WHICH ARE
OF IMMENSE SIZE, AND THE FRUIT
OF OTHERS IN VERY COMMON USE IN
THE MAKING OF PIES, WHERE HOWEVER
THEY REQUIRE THE ASSISTANCE OF
CREAM, SUGAR, NUTMEG AND OTHER
SPICES; BUT, WHEN SO PREPARED ARE
VERY PLEASANT THINGS" W. COBBETT

 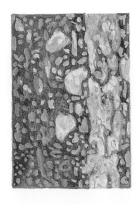 

ACORN SQUASH   GOLD STRIPED CUSHAW   TRIAMBLE

ONION SKIN
VERY
THIN
MILD WINTER
COMING
IN
ONION SKIN
THICK
AND
TOUGH
COMING WINTER
COLD
AND
ROUGH

'THE · ONION · BEING · EATEN · YEA · THOUGH · IT · BE · BOILED · ∽ CAUSETH · HEAD · ACHE · HURTETH · THE · EYES · AND · MAKETH · A · MAN · DIM · SIGHTED · DULLETH · THE · SENCES · AND · PROVOKETH · OVER · MUCH · SLEEP · ESPECIALLY · BEING · EATEN · RAW.' GERARD · 1597: AN · ONION · PEELED · OR · CUT · IN · HALF · WAS · USED · TO · DRIVE · AWAY · WITCHES : ONIONS · AND · BEANS · WILL · NOT · GROW · WELL · PLANTED · SIDE · BY · SIDE : HUNG · IN · SMOKEY · CHIMNEYS · ONIONS · WERE · THUS · PRESERVED · DURING · THE · WINTER · MONTHS ·

'THEIR · USE · IS · FITTEST · FOR · COLD · WEATHER · ∽ · AND · FOR · AGED · PHLEGMATIC · PEOPLE · WHOSE · LUNGS · ARE · STUFFED · AND · THEIR · BREATH · SHORT.' N · CULPEPER · 1826 : ONIONS · WERE · USED · BY · THE · EGYPTIANS · AS · EARLY · AS · 3000 · BC. 'MINE · EYES · SMELL · ONIONS · I · SHALL · WEEP · ANON · GOOD · TOM · DRUM · LEND · ME · A · HANKERCHEF.' SHAKESPEARE · 1603 : THE · STINGS · OF · BEES · AND · WASPS · CAN · BE · TREATED · WITH · AN · ONION · AND · SHOULD · CONSEQUENTLY · BE · PACKED · ON · A · PICNIC ·

CARROT

MEDIEVAL VARIETIES WERE PURPLE, YELLOW & WHITE. THE FERNY FOLIAGE WAS WORN BY THE COURT LADIES OF CHARLES I. IN 19TH CENTURY AMERICA CARROTS WERE GROWN MORE FOR ANIMAL FOOD THAN FOR HUMAN CONSUMPTION. "THOSE THAT WOULD GROW THIS USEFUL ROOT, FREE FROM BLIGHT AND MAGGOTS, MUST FREELY USE BOTH LIME & SOOT, AND THEY WILL HAVE FINE CARROTS."
W. GAIN 1877

SOW OUTSIDE FROM MID-SPRING IN WELL DRAINED SOIL. MANURE SHOULD BE WELL ROTTED SO THE CARROTS DO NOT BECOME FORKED.

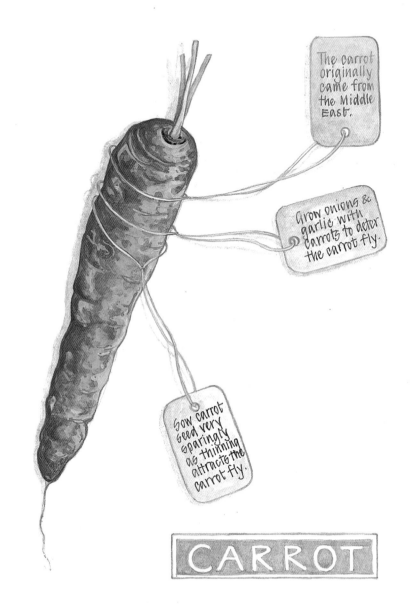

The carrot originally came from the Middle East.

Grow onions & garlic with carrots to deter the carrot fly.

Sow carrot seed very sparingly as thinning attracts the carrot fly.

CARROT

"SOME USE TO MAKE THEIR HEYRE YELOW WYTH THE
FLOURE OF THIS HERBE, NOT BEYINGE CONTENT WITH
THE NATURAL COLOUR, WHICH GOD HATH GYVEN THEM".
TURNER 1551

MARIGOLD ▫ MARIGOLD ▫

MARIGOLD ▫ MARIGOLD ▫

"THE FLOWERS EYTHER GREEN OR DRYED, ARE OFTEN
USED IN POSSETS, BROTHS, & DRINKES, AS A COMFORTER
OF THE HEART & SPIRIT." J PARKINSON 1629. CALENDULA
OR POT MARIGOLD ATTRACT HOVERFLIES WHICH EAT
APHIDS. A GOOD COMPANION PLANT WITH TOMATOES
AND CABBAGES. CALENDULA OINTMENT CURES SKIN
PROBLEMS & WAS USED TO HEAL WOUNDS IN WORLD
WAR I. JOLLY UP A GREEN SALAD WITH A SPRINKLING
OF ORANGE OR YELLOW PETALS. IT SELF SEEDS HAPPILY.

Dahlias give a wonderful splash of autumn colour with shades ranging from pale creams and soft pinks to burnt oranges and dazzling scarlets. Brought to Europe by the Spaniards from Mexico, they were later named after Dr. Dahl, a Swedish botanist. The dahlia became hugely popular in Victorian England. ° ° °

Dahlias come in many shapes — cactus, pompon, waterlily, orchid and anemone among others. Plant up tubers in pots in the spring and plant out in the garden once the frosts are over. They like sun & fertile soil. Deadhead regularly. Dig up tubers once autumn frosts arrive & dry before storing in sand. A good cut flower.

127

HYDRANGEA

HYDRANGEAS HAVE BEEN GROWN
IN JAPAN FOR CENTURIES. IT IS A
DECIDUOUS SHRUB THAT FLOWERS
FOR MANY MONTHS FROM SUMMER
TO EARLY AUTUMN. IT PREFERS A
SHADY OR SEMI-SHADY POSITION
AND MAY NEED TO BE WATERED
DURING HOT DRY SUMMERS. ON AN
ALKALINE SOIL THE FLOWERS ARE
PINK; AN ACIDIC SOIL PRODUCES
BLUE FLOWERS. OLD NAILS OR BLUE
SLATES WERE ONCE DUG IN AROUND
THE SHRUBS TO HELP PRODUCE THE
MUCH DESIRED BLUE. NOWADAYS A
BLUEING AGENT CAN BE ADDED. DO
NOT DEADHEAD UNTIL LATE THE
FOLLOWING SPRING OR FROST MAY
DAMAGE THE EMERGING BUDS.

HYDRANGEA

HYDRANGEAS DRY EXTREMELY WELL. DRY IN THE
AUTUMN ONCE THE FLOWERS ARE GOING LEATHERY
& CHANGING COLOUR. PUT THE CUT FLOWERS IN 2" OF
WATER AND LET THEM DRY SLOWLY AND NATURALLY.

129

LIGHT SUSSEX

SILVER GREY DORKING

RHODE ISLAND RED

HENS ARE CHEAP AND EASY TO KEEP PROVIDING A REGULAR SUPPLY OF FRESH EGGS, ALTHOUGH EGG PRODUCTION ALL BUT CEASES DURING THE COLDEST WINTER MONTHS. MAKE SURE THE HEN RUN IS FOX-PROOF & THE HENS ARE LOCKED UP EVERY NIGHT. FEED THE CHICKENS TWICE A DAY WITH CORN AND LAYERS PELLETS. THEY ALSO ENJOY KITCHEN SCRAPS SUCH AS RICE AND PASTA, GREENSTUFFS, GRAPES AND SUNFLOWER SEEDS BUT DO NOT GIVE THEM CITRUS FRUITS, MEAT, FISH OR EGG PRODUCTS. GIVE THEM FRESH WATER EVERY DAY. FREE RANGE THE HENS IN THE GARDEN AND THEY WILL EAT SLUGS, WEED SEEDS AND INSECTS, BUT KEEP THE HENS LOCKED IN THEIR RUN IN THE SPRING WHEN THE PLANTS IN THE GARDEN ARE SMALL & VULNERABLE. VEGETABLES MAY NEED TO BE COVERED WITH NETTING OR CLOCHES, AND THE BASE OF NEW SHRUBS AND TREES SHOULD BE PROTECTED WITH STONES. CHICKEN MANURE IS AN EXCELLENT ACTIVATOR IN THE COMPOST HEAP. MAKE SURE HENS HAVE SOME SHADE DURING HOT WEATHER. HENS MAKE A DECORATIVE ADDITION TO THE GARDEN.

·HENS IN THE GARDEN·

'SILVER DORKING'

TAKE GOOD HEEDE THAT YOUR HENNES DO NOT
SCRAPE YOUR BEDDES. L. MASCALL 1572

WINTER

WITH CHILLING COLD HAD PIERCED THE TENDER GREEN

SACKVILLE

SEASONAL TASKS

- GIVE BIRDS FOOD AND WATER
- CUT BACK DEAD STEMS OF PERENNIALS OR LEAVE UNTIL SPRING
- PLANT HEDGES
- DIG NEW BORDERS AND VEGETABLE GARDEN AND MANURE
- PLANT FRUIT TREES IN FEBRUARY AND MARCH
- CLEAN GARDEN TOOLS AND TIDY GARDEN SHED AND GREENHOUSE
- KNOCK SNOW OFF TREES AND SHRUBS
- INSPECT STORED GARDEN FRUIT AND REMOVE ROTTEN FRUIT
- PUT POTATOES IN A COOL PLACE TO 'CHIT' OR SPROUT
- STOP FEEDING FISH UNTIL SPRING
- CLEAN POND AND CLEAR OUT ANY LEAVES
- CUT DOWN NEWLY PLANTED RASPBERRY CANES TO 6" (15 CM) ABOVE THE GROUND
- PRUNE WISTERIA
- ENJOY SEED CATALOGUES AND PLAN!

WINTER

GATES

PLEASE SHUT THE GATE

PATHS PROVIDE AN ATTRACTIVE GARDEN FEATURE. EARLY PATHS WERE MADE FROM BEATEN EARTH, CINDERS OR EVEN CRUSHED SEA

SHELLS. PREPARING A GOOD FOUNDATION BASE FOR A PATH IS VITAL. PATH MATERIAL SHOULD HARMONISE WITH BOTH HOUSE AND GARDEN.

TO SIT IN THE SHADE ON A FINE DAY AND LOOK UPON VERDURE, IS THE MOST PERFECT REFRESHMENT. Jane Austen 1814

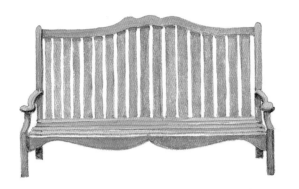

SEATING

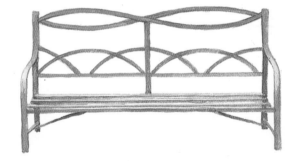
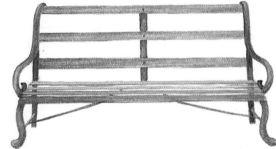

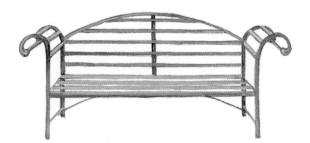

"To dig in the mellow soil — to dig moderately, for all pleasure should be taken sparingly — is a great thing."

G. Dudley Warner 1871

Digging

Digging improves the soil structure, allowing roots to grow & water to drain away.

Dig heavy soils in early winter to allow the clods to be broken down by frosts.

Adding organic matter to the soil will improve it.

Never dig when the soil is wet and sticky or it will become compacted.

Dig slowly and methodically to avoid back strain.

Use a good spade - the best is made from stainless-steel -to dig the ground, and clean it well when the job is over.

J. Loudon described digging in 1845 as "a fine healthy occupation, not only from its calling the muscles into vigorous action, but from the smell of the new earth being particularly invigorating."

Pl. XIX.

fig. 1

fig. 2

fig. 4

fig. 5

HOME-MADE COMPOST

Ingredients:

- Grass cuttings
- Straw
- Animal manure
- Kitchen scraps
- Garden waste
- Shredded newspaper

Add ingredients in thin layers. Mix well with a fork and turn frequently to speed up the cooking process.
Spread generously onto the garden when the compost has reached a crumbly consistency.
Add water if the mixture is too dry.

Ingredients to avoid:

- Diseased material – burn it.
- Cooked kitchen scraps – attract vermin
- Perennial weeds – burn them.
- Woody material – this takes too long to decompose, but it can be shredded & then added.

Comfrey, young nettles and urine are natural activators & will speed up decomposition.
"It is certainly true that dung is not the best sort of manure for a garden: it may be mixed with other matter and, if very well rotted, and almost in an earthy state, it may not be amiss."
N. CULPEPER 1833

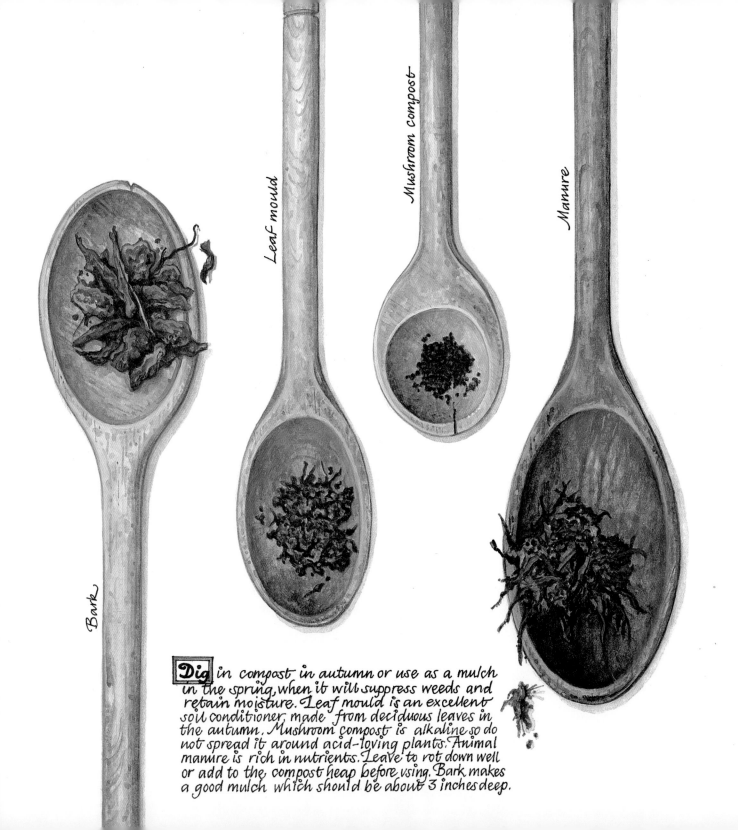

Bark

Leaf mould

Mushroom compost

Manure

Dig in compost in autumn or use as a mulch in the spring, when it will suppress weeds and retain moisture. Leaf mould is an excellent soil conditioner, made from deciduous leaves in the autumn. Mushroom compost is alkaline so do not spread it around acid-loving plants. Animal manure is rich in nutrients. Leave to rot down well or add to the compost heap before using. Bark makes a good mulch which should be about 3 inches deep.

WINTER FLOWERS · WINTER FLOWERS · WINTER FLOWERS · WINTER FLOWERS · WINTER FLOWERS · WINTER FLOWERS · WINTER FLOWERS · WINTER FLOWERS ·

· HELLEBORUS ORIENTALIS ·

· IRIS RETICULATA ·

· MAHONIA ·

· WINTER-SWEET ·

· VIBURNUM BODNANTENSE ·

· SNOWDROP ·

· HEATHER ·

· DAPHNE MEZEREUM ·

· WITCH HAZEL ·

· JASMINE ·

SNOWDROP
·GALANTHUS·

THERE ARE HUNDREDS OF VARIETIES, SOME SCENTED, DIFFERENT MARKINGS & SHAPES, SINGLE AND DOUBLE. GROWN SINCE MEDIEVAL TIMES, THEY FLOWER BETWEEN OCTOBER AND MARCH. LIFT AND DIVIDE EVERY FEW YEARS & REPLANT 'IN THE GREEN' WHEN THE LEAVES ARE DYING BACK. THEY LIKE WOODLAND CONDITIONS.

143

H HOLLY WAS PLANTED NEAR THE HOUSE TO PROTECT IT FROM LIGHTNING. SYMBOLISING ETERNAL LIFE WITH ITS EVERGREEN LEAVES IT DECORATED HOMES & CHURCHES AT XMAS.

O ONCE HARVESTED AS A NUTRITIOUS FEED FOR CATTLE AND SHEEP, THE PRICKLY LEAVES WERE ALSO USED TO CLEAN CHIMNEYS & TO BEAT CHILBLAINS WITH, TO CURE THEM.

L LEAVES BECOME LESS PRICKLY AS THE TREE AGES. THE IVORY WHITE WOOD WAS USED FOR VENEERS AND INLAYS & MADE EXCELLENT WHIPS AND MATHEMATICAL INSTRUMENTS.

L LOVELY BERRIES ARE PRODUCED BY FEMALE PLANTS. THIS TOUGH SHRUB TOLERATES COLD, STRONG WINDS, POLLUTION, SEA SPRAY AND SHADE BUT IT DOES NOT LIKE WET SOIL.

Y YELLOW, ORANGE, RED & BLACK BERRIED HOLLY CAN BE EVERGREEN OR DECIDUOUS WITH ROUND OR PRICKLY LEAVES, IT MAKES A GOOD HEDGE OR CLIPPED TOPIARY BUSH.

THERE ARE MANY DIFFERENT
VARIETIES. THIS TOUGH PLANT
WILL TOLERATE SHADE, WIND,
DROUGHT AND POLLUTION &
MAKES A GOOD HOME FOR
BIRDS AND INSECTS.

ivy
·HEDERA·

Early inns were advertised by a
bunch of ivy hanging outside ~

"IF ONE HATH GOT A SURFEIT BY DRINKING
OF WINE, HIS SPEEDIEST CURE IS TO DRINK
A DRAUGHT OF THE SAME WINE WHEREIN
A HANDFUL OF IVY LEAVES, BEING FIRST
BRUISED, HAVE BEEN BOILED." CULPEPER

A vinegar made from ivy berries was drunk
as a remedy against catching the Plague ~

Ivy was used not only to decorate
the home but also to protect it
against witchcraft & lightening.

'ON THE WHOLE, I CONSIDER IT THE MOST
DESIRABLE OF CREEPERS.' H Rider Haggard

Much topiary disappeared in the 18th century when the relaxed landscape style of Capability Brown became fashionable. Topiary became popular again with the rise of the Arts and Crafts movement and interest in the formal garden of earlier centuries.

·YEW·

·BOX·

·ROSEMARY·

·BAY·

·IVY·

·HOLLY·

·LAVENDER·

Plants chosen for topiary are usually densely leaved and slow growing, and often evergreen. Box is a favourite and was much admired by William Cobbett in 1829, "and if there be a more neat and beautiful thing than this in the world, all I can say, is, that I never saw that thing." High praise indeed!

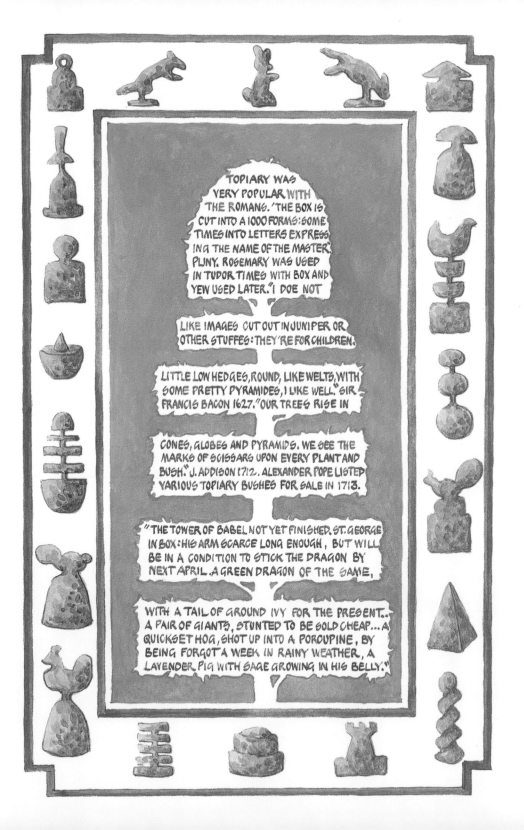

TOPIARY WAS VERY POPULAR WITH THE ROMANS. "THE BOX IS CUT INTO A 1000 FORMS: SOME TIMES INTO LETTERS EXPRESS ING THE NAME OF THE MASTER." PLINY. ROSEMARY WAS USED IN TUDOR TIMES WITH BOX AND YEW USED LATER. "I DOE NOT

LIKE IMAGES CUT OUT IN JUNIPER OR OTHER STUFFES: THEY'RE FOR CHILDREN.

LITTLE LOW HEDGES, ROUND, LIKE WELTS, WITH SOME PRETTY PYRAMIDES, I LIKE WELL." SIR FRANCIS BACON 1627. "OUR TREES RISE IN

CONES, GLOBES AND PYRAMIDS. WE SEE THE MARKS OF SCISSARS UPON EVERY PLANT AND BUSH." J. ADDISON 1712. ALEXANDER POPE LISTED VARIOUS TOPIARY BUSHES FOR SALE IN 1713.

"THE TOWER OF BABEL NOT YET FINISHED. ST. GEORGE IN BOX: HIS ARM SCARCE LONG ENOUGH, BUT WILL BE IN A CONDITION TO STICK THE DRAGON BY NEXT APRIL. A GREEN DRAGON OF THE SAME,

WITH A TAIL OF GROUND IVY FOR THE PRESENT.. A PAIR OF GIANTS, STUNTED TO BE SOLD CHEAP... A QUICKSET HOG, SHOT UP INTO A PORCUPINE, BY BEING FORGOT A WEEK IN RAINY WEATHER, A LAVENDER PIG WITH SAGE GROWING IN HIS BELLY."

·SONG THRUSH·

·GOLDFINCH·

I VALUE MY GARDEN MORE FOR THEM
BEING FULL OF BLACKBIRDS THAN
CHERRIES AND VERY FRANKLY GIVE
THEM FRUIT FOR THEIR SONGS. BY
THIS MEANS I HAVE ALWAYS THE MUSICK
OF THE SEASON IN ITS PERFECTION. J Addison 1712.

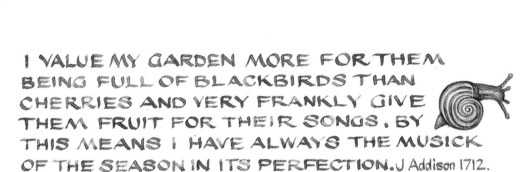

·GREAT SPOTTED WOODPECKER·

·BLACKBIRD·

THE SPARROW HATH FOUND HER AN HOUSE AND THE SWALLOW.

A NEST WHERE SHE MAY LAY HER YOUNG. PSALM EIGHTY FOUR.

NO PIGEONS

·BIRD CAKE·

Melt ½lb lard and stir into it dry ingredients such as raisins, sultanas, porridge oats, unsalted peanuts, sunflower seeds and wild bird seed. Shape into balls and wrap in plastic netting or wire mesh and hang from the bird table or the branch of a tree.

·REMEMBER TO PROVIDE WATER·

PONDS

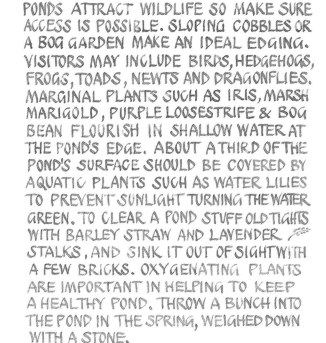

A POND SHOULD BE POSITIONED IN FULL SUN AND NOT UNDER TREES. REMOVE FALLEN LEAVES IN THE AUTUMN. THE POND SHOULD HAVE A DEPTH OF 18" (45 cm) IN SOME PLACE TO PREVENT COMPLETE FREEZING IN THE WINTER. PONDS ATTRACT WILDLIFE SO MAKE SURE ACCESS IS POSSIBLE. SLOPING COBBLES OR A BOG GARDEN MAKE AN IDEAL EDGING. VISITORS MAY INCLUDE BIRDS, HEDGEHOGS, FROGS, TOADS, NEWTS AND DRAGONFLIES. MARGINAL PLANTS SUCH AS IRIS, MARSH MARIGOLD, PURPLE LOOSESTRIFE & BOG BEAN FLOURISH IN SHALLOW WATER AT THE POND'S EDGE. ABOUT A THIRD OF THE POND'S SURFACE SHOULD BE COVERED BY AQUATIC PLANTS SUCH AS WATER LILIES TO PREVENT SUNLIGHT TURNING THE WATER GREEN. TO CLEAR A POND STUFF OLD TIGHTS WITH BARLEY STRAW AND LAVENDER STALKS, AND SINK IT OUT OF SIGHT WITH A FEW BRICKS. OXYGENATING PLANTS ARE IMPORTANT IN HELPING TO KEEP A HEALTHY POND. THROW A BUNCH INTO THE POND IN THE SPRING, WEIGHED DOWN WITH A STONE.

GOLDFISH, SHUBUNKINS, GOLDEN ORFE & KOI CARP BRING COLOUR AND
MOVEMENT TO A POND. FISH WILL BECOME TAME IF FED AT THE SAME
TIME AND PLACE EACH DAY. GIVE AS MUCH FOOD AS WILL BE EATEN
IN 20 MINUTES. DO NOT FEED IN WINTER. AQUATIC PLANTS SUCH AS
WATER LILIES PROVIDE FISH WITH SHADE AND SOMEWHERE TO HIDE.

"The gardener must not be slothful but full of zeal continuously, nor must he despise hardening his hands with toil". W Strabo c9

"But though an old man, I am but a young gardener". President T. Jefferson 1811

"The Gardener had not need be an idle or lazy Lubber... If you be not able nor willing to hire a Gardener, keep your profits to yourself, but then you must take all the pains." W Lawson 1618

"The gardener's work is never at an end; it begins with the year, & continues to the next; he prepares the ground, and then he sows it, after that he plants..." J Evelyn 1706

"TO OWN A BIT OF GROUND, TO SCRATCH IT WITH A HOE, TO PLANT SEEDS AND WATCH THEIR RENEWAL OF LIFE - THIS IS THE

COMMONEST DELIGHT OF THE RACE, THE MOST SATISFACTORY THING THAT A MAN CAN DO." C. DUDLEY WARNER 1876

RED CLOVER · BUTTERCUP · RED CAMPION

SPEEDWELL · GREATER STITCHWORT · NE

SPEEDWELL · GREATER STITCHWORT ·

LESSER CELANDINE · GREATER STITCHWORT ·

LES

RED CLOVER · BUTTERCUP · RED CAMPION

A weed is but
an unloved
flower.
Ella Wilcox 1855-1919

"WHAT MORE DELIGHTSOME
THAN AN INFINITE VARIETY
OF SWEET SMELLING FLOWERS,
DECKING WITH SUNDRY COLOURS,
THE GREEN MANTLE OF THE
EARTH." WILLIAM LAWSON 1618

160